store more, store better

No matter the size of your family or the square footage of your home, clutter is likely a part of your life. Perhaps it creeps into that messy kitchen drawer or crops up as a pile of seemingly important papers on your desk. Or maybe your entryway resembles a dumping zone, or your clothing closet begs for a top-to-bottom overhaul every time you open its door. Whether your organizing challenges are large or small, far-reaching or super-specific, *Storage with Style* has the inspiring ideas and no-fail strategies you need to conquer your clutter once and for all. Think of this book a collection of cures assembled to target your most challenging messes and chaotic spaces.

Start your de-cluttering journey by touring some homes that exemplify great storage and organization, then move on to chapters dedicated to your home's specific rooms, including kitchen, living room, dining room, bedroom, closets, bathroom, home office, entry, garage, and more. In each room-focused chapter, you'll explore ingeniously organized spaces and get detailed floor plans that map the essential zones required for smooth-working rooms. You'll also discover tons of Smart Solutions targeted to each room's specific storage challenges, such as corralling media in your living room or sorting clothes in your laundry. And because everyone loves to get something done right now, each chapter concludes with a collection of favorite Fast Fixes. These simple add-ons often improve your life quickly and inexpensively. Give one—or several—a try and see the results for yourself.

Like life, storage is all about new possibilities and fresh perspectives. Use this book to open your mind to the best organizing ideas and then open a messy cabinet or closet. Armed with dozens of stylish solutions, a less-cluttered home awaits you. Enjoy!

contents

6

22

62

Better Homes and Gard

storage
WITH STYLE

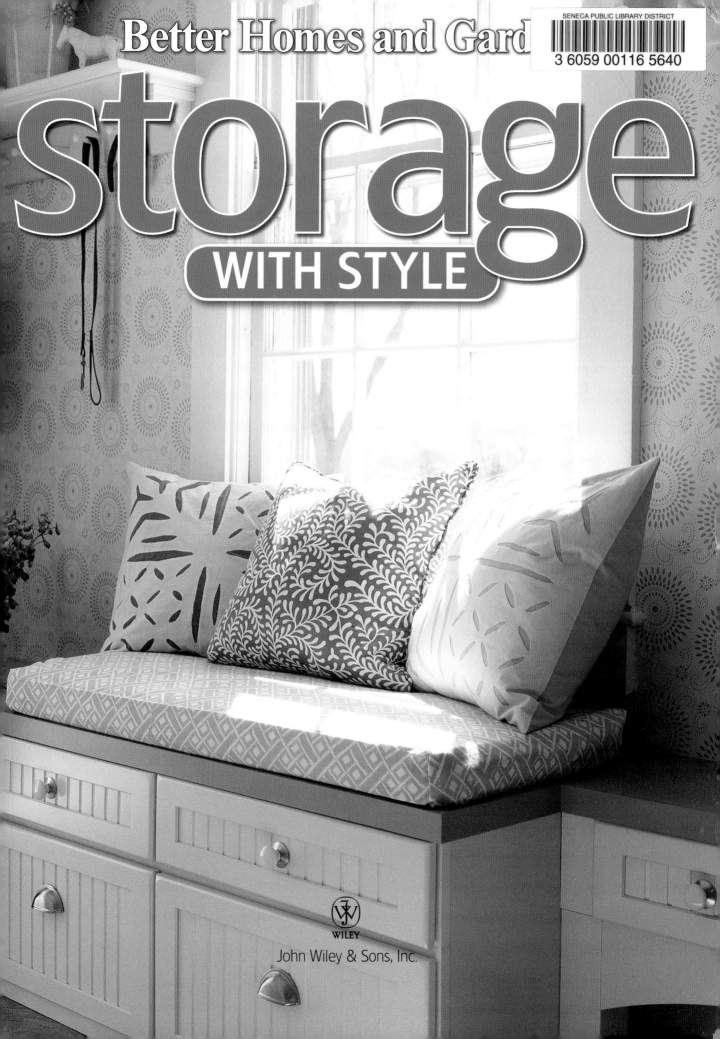

WILEY

John Wiley & Sons, Inc.

B+T
17.00

This book is printed on acid-free paper. ♾

Published by John Wiley & Sons, Inc., Hoboken, New Jersey
Published simultaneously in Canada

For general information about our other products and services, please contact our Customer Care Department within the United States at (877) 762-2974, outside the United States at (317) 572-3993 or fax (317) 572-4002.

Wiley also publishes its books in a variety of electronic formats. Some content that appears in print may not be available in electronic books. For more information about Wiley products, visit our web site at www.wiley.com.

ISBN 978-0-470-59187-1

Printed in the United States of America

10 9 8 7 6 5 4 3 2 1

92

124

150

RESOURCES PAGE 188
INSPIRED TO UPGRADE YOUR STORAGE? CHECK OUT THIS HANDY BUYING GUIDE OF TOP RETAILERS.

home
tours

FROM THE MOMENT YOU STEP INSIDE, YOU GET A SENSE OF HOW A HOME IS ORGANIZED. OF COURSE, EACH ROOM HAS ITS CHALLENGES, BUT THESE STORAGE STRATEGIES CAN IMPROVE THE FUNCTION OF ANY ROOM.

making every
inch count

Thoughtful planning boosts a home's function without adding to its footprint.

The owners of this 1954 split-level loved their suburban Chicago neighborhood but struggled to find places for their everyday possessions and favorite collections. They wanted to find architectural storage solutions without enlarging their substantial 4,000-square-foot home.

Working with an architect, they opened the dated floor plan by removing walls, enlarging passageways, and combining spaces. With each change to the floor plan, they incorporated well-designed, easy-to-use storage solutions and built-in furnishings. New open storage solutions include widened ledges for drinks and snacks in the sitting and family rooms and abundant shelving for frequently used dishware and glasses. Whenever possible, they added doors and drawers in custom built-ins and furniture, such as extra drawers in the base of the kitchen banquette and dining room window seat that links two new display hutches.

To capitalize on available space, passageways between rooms are frequently flanked with thin built-in bookcases and in the master bedroom, a grid of built-in bookcases lines a wall. Similarly, a 10×10-foot landing that could easily have been forgotten was transformed into a light-filled homework lounge. While the family lost some square footage by incorporating the new features, through this thoughtful design they gained significant function.

- **A custom ottoman/coffee table,** *this page,* designed by the homeowners provides the perfect spot to watch football or movies. The benchlike design has a rotating top with an upholstered side for feet and a hardwood side for snacks. ● **Streamlined base cabinets,** *opposite,* hide games and media, while several floating shelves display favorite collections.

IN THE DINING ROOM AND KITCHEN

● **Paint and new glass shelves,** *above* transform the dining room's traditional, basic built-ins into a sassy mod-style wall unit. ● **Glass-front upper cabinets** installed on top of a wall of windows, *opposite top,* create displaylike storage without sacrificing natural light. A slim upper band of closed cabinets capitalizes on underused space. ● **Thick passageways** between rooms, *opposite below left,* include built-in bookshelves and display space. ● **The kitchen communication center,** *opposite below right,* features a computer and a flat-panel television on an articulated arm that can be concealed behind bifold doors.

TECH FLEX

Whether you choose a custom-built communication center or purchase one from a furniture or discount store, pay attention to flexible design features. Look for work surfaces and keyboard trays that are easy to adjust in terms of height and angle. Pick cabinets and drawers that include panels or holes you can quickly punch out to accommodate cords and cables.

DO MORE

Choose or build a bookcase with fully finished sides and rear panel. That way you can position the unit anywhere in a room and have it function as a room divider, serving buffet, console table, or backing for bench-style seating. Attach rubber feet to ensure the piece stays put on hard flooring.

IN THE BREAKFAST NOOK

● **A partial wall and bookcase unit,** *opposite,* bridges the kitchen and sitting room and holds cookbooks, magazines, and the children's essential toys (in color-coded bins). ● **Red birch banquette seating** in the kitchen, *top,* was selected for its cozy 1950s feel and hosts kids or guests while the cook prepares meals. The freestanding red birch table was also custom-made to maximize seating. ● **Drawers under the bench,** *above,* hold place mats and napkins. With long handles and smooth-gliding tracks, they're designed to be kid-accessible, so young ones can help out.

SITTING PRETTY

Beds and benches are typically 24
to 30 inches off the ground and feature
significant untapped storage potential beneath
the upholstered surface or mattress. Add skirting
or hang fabric panels to mask less-than-lovely
items—or use the space to show off durable items
such as books, toys, stuffed animals, pillows, or
blankets. Subdivide the space with risers or
platform-style shelves; then organize with
a mix of baskets, bins, and boxes.

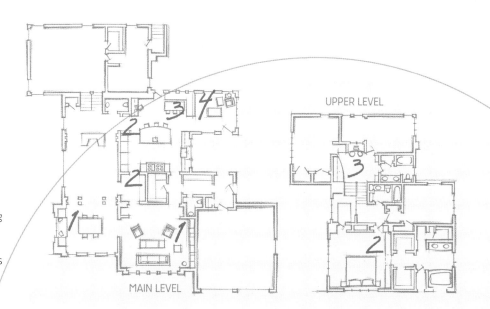

UPPER LEVEL

MAIN LEVEL

IN THE BEDROOMS

● **The homework lounge** on the landing outside the children's relatively small bedrooms, *opposite,* packs function into a once-forgotten space. Book storage wraps under and above a curvy built-in couch that comfortably accommodates two young readers or one catnapping adult. ● **The computer nook,** *opposite below,* occupies a sliver of space between the bedroom doors. An interior window pulls natural light from one bedroom. Sized for a "pilot and copilot" while surfing the Internet, the space can be reconfigured as the homeowners' daughters grow.
● **12-inch-deep bookcases** in the master bedroom, *below,* are perfect for passionate readers. A notched cubby at the top of the unit adds a special spot to showcase favorite collectibles.

IN THE ZONE
Clever tricks make the most of available square footage.

1 wrap
Lining entire walls with bookcases, cabinets, or open shelving may have sacrificed strips of square feet but resulted in abundant new storage.

2 widen
18- to 24-inch-wide passageways display books and collections in open shelves and store electronics and less-used appliances in lower, closed compartments.

3 sit
More than mere structures to hold stuff, upholstered tops on window seats, banquettes, and the custom coffee table serve as inviting spots to kick back.

4 divide
Islands and partial walls separate spaces (and offer loads of space to stash stuff). But at 30 to 36 inches tall, these features still allow casual interaction.

double up
on function

Custom storage pieces do more and put this home at the top of its class.

Not every home is born with great storage. A limited floor plan, nearly 100 years of wear and tear, and several previous remodel projects had stripped this rectangular Victorian house in Chicago of most of its character—and left the homeowners with limited storage options. The owners sought out and hired an interior designer with extensive experience integrating stylish and functional storage. Satisfying needs and introducing innovative ideas, the designer added closets, shelves, cabinets, and double-duty furniture pieces to create a place for everything in the home.

One of the project's most successful strategies was incorporating furniture that serves more than one function. For example, the dining area, dressed up with a new padded bench and dramatic walnut-stained sideboard, is also the family's home office. The cabinets of the sideboard open into a desk, while large drawers below the banquette mask legal-size hanging files. Other cabinets corral infrequently used vases and office supplies. When work is done and it's time to play, everything closes and the corner becomes a cozy spot to read, play a board game, or relax with friends.

Most of the custom storage required sacrificing some floor space—a tough call in a narrowly designed home like this one—but the additions exponentially increased each room's organization and capacity. For example, adding a pair of closets and a low cabinet around the perimeter of the family room took up a $1\frac{1}{2}$-foot band of space, but the alteration eliminated clutter and gave the family a gathering spot for coats, toys, and backpacks.

IN THE LIVING ROOM

● **Twin bookshelves,** *this page,* fill a formerly empty wall, creating plenty of space for the homeowners' extensive library. ● **Extra cabinets** below the shelves house file drawers for legal documents and paperwork. ● **A new, large mantel** creates a sleek spot for favorite works of art and frames the focal point fireplace. ● **A slim console table,** *opposite,* serves as display ledge for art and flowers.

TRIM TRICK

Only 14 inches deep, this custom bench hugs the dining room wall while still affording considerable storage for files and papers in three broad drawers. Use similarly shallow thinking in your bedroom or closet; fill a bookcase with folded clothing, shoes, bins of socks, or baskets of accessories.

IN THE DINING ROOM

● **Built-ins and bench seating,** *above,* wrap around a circular dining table, offering a range of seating, display, and storage opportunities. ● **Closed cabinets,** *below left,* under the bookshelves house decorating and entertaining essentials. ● **Large drawers,** *below center,* under the bench are the perfect for organizing files and paperwork. ● **A corner cabinet,** *below right,* keeps boxes of extra office supplies close at hand. ● **A built-in hutch,** *opposite,* opens to form a desk area. The computer screen slips into a closed cabinet, and the keyboard pushes under the counter. A roll-out drawer extends for access to the printer/scanner/fax machine when in use.

IN THE KITCHEN & BREAKFAST NOOK

● **Shallow floor-to-ceiling shelves,** *left,* built into the wall of the breakfast nook create space for storing tableware. ● **A large island** in the kitchen, *below,* boosts the storage in a room with limited wall space. The piece adds a substantial work surface without interrupting the room's flow.

IN THE FAMILY ROOM

● **Two tall corner closets,** *above left,* take advantage of previously unused space and add architectural interest to the family room. They also create a spot to trap potential clutter, such as jackets, shoes, backpacks, and board games. ● **A long storage cabinet,** *above right,* lines one wall, replacing a bulky armoire-style entertainment center. A mix of reed and wicker baskets in the lower cabinets hold art supplies, books, games, and media.

IN THE ZONE
Sneak in clever storage throughout the home.

1 fill
Take advantage of underused corners and slim strips of floor space by building in compact closets and shallow floor-to-ceiling shelving with closed lower cabinets.

2 double up
Combine functions for furniture (such as a built-in that serves as both bench and file cabinet) and rooms (a space that does home office and dining room duties).

3 open
Remove walls, doors, and other physical and visual barriers between spaces. Open spaces feel more connected and boost both spaces' function.

4 update
If old cabinets or closets don't meet your needs, it's time for a change. Add new shelves, baskets, or doors to bolster the style and function of rooms.

kitchen
spaces

EQUAL PARTS EFFICIENT AND BEAUTIFUL, KITCHEN
STORAGE MAKES STOCKING FOOD, PREPARING MEALS, AND DINING DELIGHTFUL
EXPERIENCES. RELY ON THIS CHAPTER FOR DOZENS OF INNOVATIVE SOLUTIONS.

cooking for
a crowd

Hardworking storage makes efficient, professional-style preparation its focus.

Designed for a cook who embraces the challenge of preparing large or intricate dishes—and considers entertaining an art form—this meticulously executed space places the range (and cook) at center stage with myriad sensible and accessible storage components all around. Within arm's reach and tucked under the range hood is a handy spice rack and a clever organizational system for food prep that the French refer to as a *mise en place*. The restaurant-inspired staging concept consists of cutouts in the counter that hold metal storage bins in assorted sizes and provide convenient storage for items including dry goods and wooden spoons. A vintage double sink with two faucets provides the organizing feature for the cleanup zone, where a wall-mount plate rack keeps everyday dinnerware close to the dishwasher.

In lieu of a walk-in pantry, an entire wall is dedicated to food and beverage storage. Glass-front cabinets housing jars and packaged goods flank a full-service coffee bar, a microwave hides behind a handsome tambour door, and a pair of extra-long cabinet doors open to reveal handy roll-out trays and swinging racks. Furniture-style islands provide dual functions: One can host informal dining, and the other offers overflow food-prep space. In the latter, a second *mise en place* lets busy home chefs prepare and store recipe ingredients ahead of time—or set up a self-serve bar for sundaes, salads, tacos, or omelets. And for catered affairs, the self-contained butler's pantry offers an out-of-sight staging area with a full complement of appliances, stylish open storage for china and glassware, and a baking center in between.

THIS PHOTO: Variable-height shelving by the stove works for all manner of spice jars. Dish towels hang in an open cabinet by the sink. OPPOSITE: Concealed shelving, conveniently located next to the stove, glides out to reveal serving pieces and cast-iron cookware.

● **Two walls of well-placed cabinets,** deep drawers, and varied open shelving, *far left,* wrap the kitchen in a broad range of storage options. ● **A tambour door,** *left,* functions like a roll-top desk, lifting to reveal a toaster and breakfast supplies. Open shelves above organize cookbooks, while wicker bins corral recipe cards. ● **Glass-front cabinets** and open storage, *below,* surround the beverage station. Baskets in open lower cabinets hold produce and slide out for easy use.

Two islands—one for the cook, the other for guests—allow for both unity and specialized zoning. It's a combination that satisfies everyone.

● **A section of open shelving,** *opposite,* squeezes between a pair of wall ovens and a French-door refrigerator, allotting a spot in the butler's pantry for cake- and pie-making necessities. ● **A custom oak china hutch,** *left,* displays pretty pitchers, plates, teapots, and serving pieces. ● **Removable metal bins** in assorted sizes set into the solid-surface countertops, *above,* keep cooking implements close at hand. ● **More metal bins** set into the food-prep island, *above right,* keep recipe ingredients at the ready or can function as a toppings buffet for salads or sundaes.

IN THE ZONE

Professional-style details support a passionate home chef.

1 prep
Near the range, this island sports a sink for washing vegetables, drawers for frequently used utensils, and a shelf below for storing mixing bowls and baskets of ingredients.

2 cook
Glass-front cabinets, open shelves, *mise en place* bins, and an appliance garage arranged along a single strip of floor space put essentials at the cook's fingertips.

3 host
A second island surrounded by space-saving stools lets guests chat with the chef or gather for a casual meal. Wire baskets on low shelves stow table linens.

4 drink
A refrigerator and icemaker below and coffee-making accoutrements above encourage guests to help themselves to warm and cool beverages.

5 stow
Special pieces hold clusters of culinary gear: A hutch holds serving pieces, open racks organize dishes, and a cabinet in the butler's pantry is dedicated to baking.

comfort and.
convenience

Major floor plan changes transform a suburban kitchen into a beautiful workroom.

When style trumps substance, especially in the kitchen, problems with function seem to magnify with time. For the owners of this kitchen, the original design was simply too small—an undersize sink, inadequate countertops, and, most troubling, meager and unimaginative storage. So after consulting with an architect, an architectural designer, an interior designer, and a contractor, the homeowners began an extensive redesign of the kitchen and adjacent spaces, which now encompass a substantial butler's pantry, a beverage center, and a breakfast area.

Priorities for the main area ranged from grouping the major appliances to devising specific storage solutions for an array of appliances and accessories. Banks of cabinets extend to the 10-foot-high ceiling, creating an abundance of additional space. A stepladder helps cooks reach seldom-used items stored high, such as picnic supplies and holiday dishes.

Designed to look like a piece of vintage furniture, the new island, 6 inches lower than the other countertops to accommodate children, serves as the primary prep area. The bilevel peninsula, meanwhile, contains a dishwasher, dishwasher drawers, and a generous farmhouse sink. Visually, the large piece creates even more impact, separating the kitchen from the living area while still allowing openness. Steps away, the butler's pantry is a marvel of well-planned storage. Base cabinets conceal containers and supplies as well as amenities such as a bread drawer. Overhead shelves place sundries within comfortable reach and in sight. Function, beauty, and style—few cooks could ask for more.

• **The corner beverage center,** *opposite,* includes a built-in refrigerator, ice maker, and wine cooler, in addition to ample countertop space to double as a serving station. • **Deep pullout drawers,** *left,* flank the range and ensure that the right cookware is never out of arm's reach. • **A two-tier undercounter pullout,** *above left,* uses formerly wasted corner space to house food processors and coffee carafes that might have been banished to the pantry. • **Drawers fitted with stainless-steel dividers,** *above right,* keep the designated area for flatware and other utensils neat and tidy. As another time-saving design, the drawers are located near the dishwasher. • **Stair-stepped spice storage,** *below,* in an upper cabinet near the range displays dozens of canisters in clear, easy-to-access rows.

Reorganizing the appliances and storage features into focused work zones gives the kitchen a layout that looks great and functions beautifully.

● **A combination of shallow and deep drawers** in the butler's pantry, *opposite*, makes for truly customized storage solutions. ● **Open, adjustable shelves**, *left*, give the homeowners a clear view of what's in their larder. ● **An old-fashioned bread drawer** with a ventilated lid, *above*, was inspired by one of the homeowners' grandmother's kitchen. ● **Custom cubbies** tailored to the size of the homeowners' cookware, *above right*, may mean additional initial cost, but having a specific place for each major kitchen item yields efficiency and minimizes clutter and confusion.

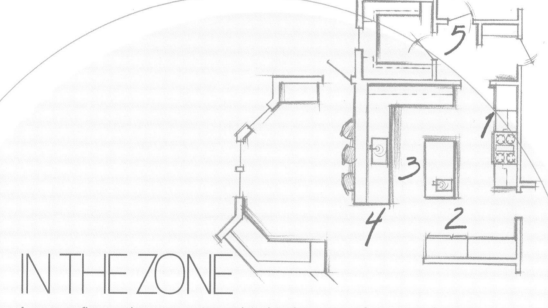

IN THE ZONE

A savvy floor plan organizes this kitchen into functional areas.

1 cook
Slatted inserts in cabinets next to the oven hold cookie sheets and cutting boards, while self-closing drawers by the range keep the area clear and safe.

2 drink
Guests can access the refrigerator, icemaker, and wine cooler without hampering the cook. Glass-front upper cabinets showcase stemware.

3 prep
The 30-inch-tall central island is 6 inches shorter than surrounding counters, topped with hardwood for chopping, and outfitted with a vegetable sink.

4 eat
The bar side of the peninsula is elevated 8 inches to subtly divide the kitchen from the breakfast area and to hide barstools when not in use.

5 store
Base cabinets conceal storage containers and kitchen supplies, while four rows of open shelves above keep foodstuffs in easy reach.

zoned for
performance

Storage pieces grouped by function streamline an expansive retro kitchen.

This family-friendly kitchen incorporates carefully thought-out spaces for cooking, baking, eating, relaxing, and working. Base storage units tie all the areas of the U-shape room together, while drawers outfitted with custom racks and dividers organize appliances, pots, and pans out of sight. Along the back wall, open shelving displays dishes. At the low-counter baking station, more open shelving holds cookie jars, while baking utensils dangle from a wall holder.

Close to a cheeky red banquette, pantry cupboards and a freestanding cabinet contain additional self-service centers. Open shelving above the banquette stores reference materials, cookbooks, and a collection of globes that stands ready to assist with homework. A nook beneath the shelves forms a garage for a custom cart stocked with craft supplies. In the extra-deep window seat across from the banquette, the theme is relaxation. Oversize drawers and shelving contain comforts for kids and adults: games, books, toys, blankets, and a flat-panel television. Curtains in front of the seat can even be closed for snatching a quick snooze. The adjacent mudroom offers more attractive storage with a low shower to house muddy clothes and boots, plus semicustom cabinetry outfitted with cubbies and bins to function like a no-nonsense mail room for the whole family.

THIS PHOTO: Glass cookie jars at the rounded kitchen bar counter encourage snacking and conversation, while open shelves hold frequently used, display-worthy items. OPPOSITE: Base cabinets follow the length of the U-shape kitchen.

- **A freestanding armoire,** *opposite,* holds party and homework supplies. Different door panels and a darker finish distinguish it from the rest of the cabinetry. The vibrant red quartz bar floats above the soapstone-look countertops, offering guests at the diner-style stools a few more inches of legroom. ● **An inset upholstered window seat** with drawers sized for toys and shelves scaled for board games, *left,* doubles as a cozy spot for a catnap. ● **Pop-up cantilevered shelves,** *above left,* allow easy access to heavy baking appliances ● **Open shelving with streamlined brackets,** *above right,* holds everyday dishware and contrasts with the chalkboard-paint backsplash. ● **In the baking center,** *below,* a wall rack with S-hooks keeps necessities in easy reach, while open shelving showcases an eclectic mix of cookie jars ready for fresh baked goods.

Each zone in this retro-style kitchen houses and organizes the utensils, appliances, and ingredients required to work on specific tasks from start to finish.

● **Curved wall shelves,** *opposite,* mimic the bean-shape island counter. A collection of globes and reference materials is handy for busy students. ● **A nook** behind the banquette, *left,* stores a rolling cart for art and homework projects. ● **A freestanding multipurpose cabinet** with adjustable shelves, *above left,* accommodates oversize items such as platters, games, books, and media equipment. Matching baskets on the pullout shelf act as catchalls. ● **A narrow shelf** above the low shower, *above right,* makes a handy perch for cleaners and brushes for dirty feet, paws, or boots.

IN THE ZONE

Whatever a family wants to do, this kitchen offers a special spot.

1 work
This tile-covered corridor deftly organizes family mail and gear in built-in cabinets and provides an easy-care area for hanging wet stuff and grooming pets.

2 gather
The cheery banquette area hosts meals, homework, and art projects thanks to flexible shelving and a supply cart that slips between the built-in unit and the wall.

3 cook
Meal prep is a breeze around the two-sink, L-shape central island. A curvy snack bar floats above the work area and offers perching spots for up to four guests.

4 snack
A baking/snack area at the edge of the cook zone, near the wall oven and microwave, lets family members serve themselves without getting in the chef's way.

5 relax
A cushioned window seat with shelves, privacy curtains, and a TV niche provides a comfy spot to lounge while still being part of the room's activities.

smart solutions
islands

Pack this central spot for meal preparation with a bevy of practical features.

1 VERSATILE DESIGN In this L-shape island, open shelves display baskets and copper cookware, while drawers hide less attractive items. The taller counter offers more storage space below—and hides dirty dishes at the sink.

2 SPICE IT UP A shallow cabinet at one end of this prep area keeps spices and oils within easy reach of the cook.

3 ENTERTAINMENT ZONE Open shelving on this island offers plenty of space for cookbooks and transforms the adjacent breakfast nook into a prime TV-watching spot.

4 DEFINING DETAILS Wire baskets hold produce and offer a farm-fresh look. Scrollwork on the island echoes the vintage theme, while an electrical outlet hidden at one side ensures modern convenience.

small-space strategy No room for an island? Use a kitchen cart instead. It can serve as an extra prep area, and many models feature drawers, shelves, and hooks for storing supplies. Most are on wheels, so you can easily move them as needed.

1

smart solutions
pantries

Organize cooking staples and canned goods for easy-in, easy-out efficiency.

1 LONG, TALL BEAUTY In addition to traditional upper and lower cabinetry, include a single cabinet with French doors in a kitchen. Look for extra-tall units from semicustom cabinetry manufacturers, convert a freestanding wardrobe, or (as in this kitchen) work with a carpenter to build in an armoire-style piece. For a vintage-inspired look, choose paneled doors, glass inserts, and fabric liners.

2 ON THE SLIDE If you don't have room to accommodate a swinging pantry, consider accessing the storage area via a pocket door that disappears into the wall.

3 CURVE APPEAL Floor-to-ceiling lazy Susans ensure that everything is accessible in a corner pantry. A gently bowing door softens the unit's angles and injects streamlined style.

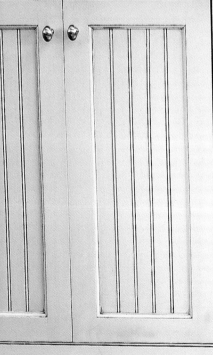

smart solutions
cook stations

Store your culinary tools and supplies where you use them most.

1 IN PLAIN SIGHT Open drawers below a cooktop roll out for quick access while you cook and keep your hardest working pots and pans clearly organized.

2 NIFTY NICHE Put the area behind the range to work with a built-in niche. It's the perfect spot for storing oils and spices.

3 ON THE COUNTERTOP Knife slots in the countertop are conveniently placed in the prep area—without taking up valuable work space. Nearby, a wall-mounted spool of string makes tying up a chicken or roast fast and easy.

4 HANGING AROUND Make the most of limited space in a small kitchen by taking advantage of bare walls under cabinets. Copper cookware hangs from S-hooks on a backsplash rail, offering convenience and style.

group like with like As you organize your kitchen, cluster the tools, appliances, supplies, and foodstuffs that you use simultaneously. For example, store mugs and bowls as well as cereals and breads near your coffeemaker, toaster, or juicer.

smart solutions
tight spots

Squeeze more function into unexpected spaces with these smart strategies.

1 LOOK UP When you can't find enough storage space, think vertically. This slim pantry packs lots of storage into a narrow strip between a refrigerator and a china cabinet.

2 CLEVER CUBBIES An efficient wine storage area can fit into the smallest of spaces. In this kitchen, a vertical row of cubbies stores wine next to a column of basket drawers.

3 FILLER IDEAS A narrow base cabinet is just the right size to accommodate those awkward platters that don't seem to fit anywhere. Or use similarly oriented cabinets to organize baking sheets, muffin pans, or cutting boards.

4 DOUBLE DUTY A shelf tucked above the bins inside this recycling center cabinet stores trash bags right where they're needed.

clever disguises The best storage features hide their hardworking function behind a designer front. For example, the trash and recycling center, *above*, is discreetly tucked away behind a cabinet panel designed to look like three vintage-style drawers.

smart solutions
open shelving

Rather than hide your prettiest kitchen things, put them on display and enjoy.

2

3

1 ABOVE THE SINK Install a shelving unit above the cleanup area to re-create the charm of an old-fashioned hutch. Bold green paint, tongue-and-groove backing, and scallop trim complement the display of antique dishes.

2 IN THE PANTRY Sturdy wrought-iron brackets lend decorative appeal to the simple shelves that wrap around the walls of this hardworking storage closet. A background of hand-painted stripes reinforces the room's vintage style.

3 AROUND THE RANGE Painted shelves frame the range hood to create a budget-friendly focal point. Store serving pieces and baskets on upper shelves, and reserve lower shelves for everyday plates and mugs.

smart solutions inside cabinets

Outfit drawers and more with clever accessories that control kitchen chaos.

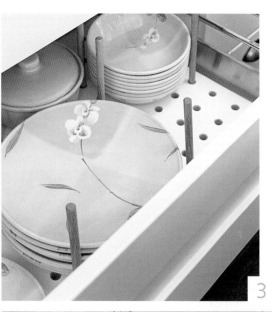

1 HOT RODS Remove interior cabinet shelves and then mount wood dowels to the side walls using window treatment hardware. Drape table linens and dish cloths over the dowels for wrinkle-free storage.

2 REPURPOSED RACK After nesting all your plastic containers, file the lids in an unused CD rack to keep drawers clutter-free.

3 PEGGED IN PLACE Storing dishes in low drawers near a sink or dishwasher minimizes overhead lifting. Peg-and-board inserts can be sized to fit existing drawers and adjusted to secure stacks of bowls and plates.

4 WIRE WONDER When this cabinet opens, an interlocking series of stainless-steel racks unfolds, pulling pots and pans forward from deep within a corner cabinet.

if you only have one hour...

Take inventory of a drawer or cabinet, because you don't need to store things you don't use. Toss plastic containers that are cracked, warped, or missing lids. Purge any pot or pan you haven't used in the past year.

smart solutions
backsplashes

Designate the walls behind the range, sink, or counter for often-used items.

1 LINED UP Staggered wall shelves take a style cue from the graphic tile backsplash and extend open storage and display space for dishes all the way to the ceiling.

2 INSET INGENUITY Carving out space between wall studs introduces a shallow spot for shelves. Fill a niche near the range with frequently used spices, oils, and measuring devices; near the sink, store dish detergent, sponges, or drinking glasses.

3 PARALLEL POISE Inspired by hard-working restaurant kitchens, stainless-steel shelves and utensils with curved handles dangle from a wall-mount rack.

4 HOOK AND COOK A framed piece of pegboard outfitted with repositionable hooks and brackets organizes a bevy of kitchen gear.

⏱ if you only have one hour...
Hang a towel bar on your sink backsplash, about 6 to 12 inches above the countertop—or a few inches below the bottom of the upper cabinets. Drape dish towels or hang kitchen accessories from S-hooks.

smart solutions
tableware
Keep mealtime essentials organized with these clever ideas.

1 LOAD UP ON LINENS Unified with a coat of cream spray paint, willow baskets on open shelves become the perfect solution to organize place mats, dish towels, napkins, and other table linens.

2 BAR AREA Display stemware in an unused corner to create an entertainment zone that encourages guests to help themselves.

3 DISHES ON DISPLAY Colorful plates stored in a built-in plate rack bring a decorative note to the kitchen—and make quick work of setting the table.

4 SILVERWARE BINS This custom drawer turns traditional storage upside down by standing flatware on end, so it's easy to grab by the handles. If custom cabinets aren't in the budget, group utensils in countertop canisters.

formal dining Special-occasion dinnerware deserves specialty storage. Place sterling silver flatware in drawers lined with Pacific Silvercloth, which prevents tarnishing. Keep tablecloths on pullout cedar dowel rods to keep the fabric wrinkle- and moth-free.

smart solutions
small appliances

Stash these essential kitchen tools in creative, easy-to-access spots.

1 SNACK BAR Keep food prep accessories out of the way but close at hand by designating a cabinet as a breakfast area or snack bar. Locate frequently used appliances, such as a toaster, in a prominent spot and place less-used appliances on lower shelves. Install electrical outlets inside the cabinet and include a pullout shelf for safety.

2 HEAVY LOAD Lifting some appliances onto the counter can be a chore—unless you plan ahead. Built-in cantilevered shelves easily raise a food processor to counter height and tuck it away when you're finished.

3 COFFEE CENTER Streamline your morning routine with a handy coffee center. An open shelf on the upper cabinet keeps mugs and cereal bowls near your morning java.

14 fast fixes: pantry

Indulge your passion for cakes and cookies with a designated zone for baking gear.

solutions:

1 House aprons, dish towels, mitts, and even a rolling pin on an over-the-door wire-hook unit.

2 Rest a shoe riser on a shelf and gain another layer of storage.

3 Ensure everything will return to the right spot with repositionable vinyl labels.

4 Corral an array of mini pans and cookie cutters in a clear container.

5 Utilize every cubic inch of space with square or rectangular (rather than round) vessels.

6 Arrange supplies on a stairstep-style rack for easy access.

7 Position beaters and other tools on cup hooks screwed into the underside of a shelf.

8 Consolidate waxed paper, foil, and paper towel storage in a single wall-mount dispenser.

9 Replace lower shelves with a work cart that houses heavy appliances.

10 Hang dish towels from an over-the-cabinet-door hook.

11 Outfit a drawer with plastic dividers and elevated inserts to organize small ingredients and tools.

12 Fill clear-top plastic containers with sprinkles and spices.

13 Orient cutting boards, trays, and baking sheets vertically with rubber-coated wire racks.

14 Use shower curtain hardware to suspend measuring tools from a towel bar.

living
spaces

KICKING BACK TO SNACK OR RELAX IS MORE SATISFYING WHEN YOUR ROOMS ARE WELL-ORGANIZED. THIS CHAPTER OFFERS IDEAS YOU CAN IMPLEMENT IMMEDIATELY IN YOUR FAMILY, LIVING, AND DINING ROOMS.

multifunctional
family room

An energetic, versatile design puts entertainment and comfort front and center.

In this cheeky basement family room, entertainment and play items abound, but clever cover-ups keep the space from feeling cluttered or disorganized. In the sitting area, a coffee table chest supports weary feet and stows blankets. Six sheer panels attached to window-treatment tracks draw back to unveil a fully loaded media center. Within this niche, bracketed shelves hold board games and display items, while a band of horizontal storage cubbies hold CDs and DVDs. A row of glass-front cabinets holds more items in vibrant green bins. A series of benches outfitted with open shelves and drawers lines the adjacent wall, providing seating for guests and nooks to stash toys, books, and pillows. Rolling side tables offer additional drawer space and move-to-order surfaces for enjoying food or playing games.

Tucked around the corner, a commercial-grade worktable outfitted with a sink conveniently functions as a bar just a few steps from the popular gathering area. A metal-look laminate panel hung on a door slider conceals the plumbing but can be pushed aside for access to crates and a wine cooler. Textured baskets add color and make it effortless to move drink accessories—such as coasters and napkins—to the countertop or sitting area. The contemporary shelves were made by purchasing brackets and custom-cut glass, which cost a fraction of the price of look-alike retail items. On a nearby wall, a console table outfitted with woven baskets and glass canisters displays treasured vacation mementos and guides for planning the next fun and exciting adventure.

THIS PHOTO: Wheeled bench storage units coordinate with eye-popping walls and offer open spots and drawers for stashing books and games.
OPPOSITE: A simple maple console table shows off glass canisters containing travel mementos. Baskets below hold pamphlets, guides, and books.

An on-the-go family needs furniture that moves and **adapts** to its ever-evolving needs. Sliding screens and wheeled storage cubes fill the bill.

- **Bracketed wall shelves,** horizontal storage cubbies, and home-theater console tables, *opposite,* organize a wealth of media and display favorite art and photos.
- **Six sheer panels,** *left,* attached to three window-treatment tracks slide closed to conceal the television area. Fabric letters and numbers applied with fusible webbing and secured with whipstitches enliven the plain material. • **Side table drawers,** *above left,* are each drilled with a simple hole to use as a pull; for added convenience, the drawers slide out on either side of the unit. • **A commercial-grade worktable,** cut to hold a vessel sink, *above right,* supports a wine cooler and crates. Barware rests on glass shelves above.

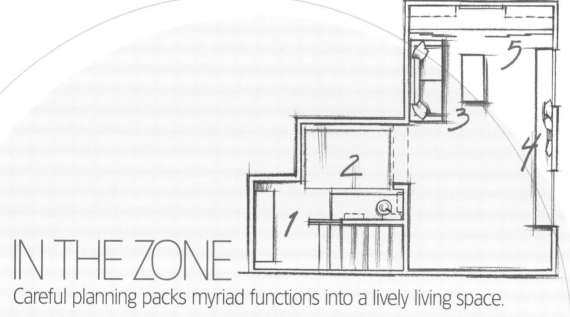

IN THE ZONE

Careful planning packs myriad functions into a lively living space.

1 display
This area at the bottom of the stairs serves as a tribute to the family's passion for world travel. Shelves and baskets hold guides and maps to plan future adventures.

2 party
A wet bar outfitted with a cooler and topped by wall shelving sports everything necessary to get good times rolling, including glasses, beverages, and baskets of supplies.

3 lounge
A comfy couch encourages folks to unwind and watch movies. A coffee table chest hides blankets and board games and provides a spot to prop up feet.

4 play
Four wheeled cubes give each family member a spot to store favorite toys, books, or games. Upholstered tops and pillows let the units function as versatile seating, too.

5 watch
Panels mask a flat-screen television surrounded by wall shelves and cubbies. Three off-the-rack media consoles span the space like a single custom storage unit.

the ultimate
media cabinet

This two-sided Craftsman-style built-in is equal parts work and play.

Multipurpose spaces require hardworking furniture, and these demands can yield disappointingly utilitarian results. Fortunately, the owners of this family room were able to collaborate with their builder and architect to create a multi-function built-in that earns high marks for both style and substance.

The work side of this maple-and-mahogany-accented unit centers around a stone-topped work surface where a busy parent can dash off an e-mail or a child can tend to homework. Recessed can lights and a table lamp provide a comfortable mix of ambient and task lighting, while the slab countertop features routed holes along its back edge for myriad cords and cables. A ledge to the right of the workstation serves as a secondary spot for spreading out supplies or reading material and wraps around to the unit's media-centric side.

Elevated two steps from the work area, the media room utilizes the cabinet's generous dimensions to organize a bevy of electronics and entertaining accessories. Three drawers along the base hide blankets and a gaming system, while a trio of compartments above hold media and electronic components. A large flat-panel television fills the upper compartment, which features hinged doors that tuck inside the cabinet box for uninterrupted viewing from anywhere in the room.

THIS PHOTO: Although substantial, this maple built-in allows natural light and sound to cross from the media area to the work space beyond, allowing privacy while encouraging casual interaction. OPPOSITE: A step below the media area, the work side of the unit features a stone work surface and generous legroom.

sophisticated
gathering space

Work, dining, and relaxation harmoniously cohabit in this lovely, efficient room.

Who knew an ultrafunctional living space could look so charming? Gliding beneath a lavish bank of windows, custom cabinetry finished with chamfered edges doubles as a home office by day and an expansive glass-top buffet by night. The drawers house tools and supplies and conceal a hinged drafting table, while the flexible design allows rearranging. Wall nooks fitted with adjustable shelves cover the opposite side of the room; each shelf's height matches its contents. Short shelves support wire racks labeled for quick reference, while slightly taller shelves stow translucent boxes, stacked books, and pottery and double-high shelves make way for a set of Asian jars.

Simply elegant furniture turns the living area into an inviting and functional retreat. Caned chairs decked with comfy cushions surround a glass-top table ideal for writing letters, holding meetings, or dining. A plush chenille armchair paired with a coordinating oversize ottoman invites curling up with a book. To further optimize storage, items are grouped by scenario. A silver tray loaded with message-taking tools sits at arm's reach from the phone. Labeled drawer dividers keep items separate yet coordinated, and color-coordinated files quickly identify categories such as finances and vacations.

THIS PHOTO: Wire baskets and translucent boxes stowed in the built-ins group like items while keeping them visible.
OPPOSITE: Roses gathered in a glass vase complement the soft beauty of this multipurpose living area.

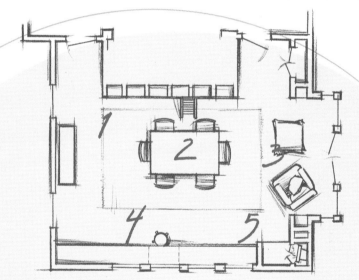

● **A bank of glass-top cabinetry,** *opposite,* beautifully stores office supplies and doubles as a serving buffet. ● **Dividers labeled by contents,** *left,* keep items within distinct areas and make it easy for anyone in the household to find or replace supplies.

● **Tall bookshelves that match the French doors' height and finish,** *above left,* create unity in the room. The chenille chair and ottoman roll to accommodate reading, snacking, or watching TV. ● **Glass jars filled with colorful office necessities,** *above right,* function as delicious, organized eye candy.

IN THE ZONE

Careful planning packs myriad functions into a lush living space.

1 organize
Floor-to-ceiling shelving sorts books, projects, and collections in an array of boxes, baskets, and bins. A rolling library ladder makes upper shelves accessible.

2 gather
The glass-top table can comfortably seat six diners. With the addition of a lamp and a tray of office supplies, the table quickly converts to an expansive desk.

3 read
Transom-top French doors flood this reading niche with light and views. Two slim bookcases built into the side walls claim easily forgotten space.

4 work
This run of cabinets includes partitioned drawers and a hinged drafting table. An efficient rolling stool can tuck away when the cabinets are used as a serving buffet.

5 relax
A corner cluster of upper cabinets frees up views and discretely houses entertainment equipment, including a flat-panel television and stereo.

designed for
good times

A pair of laid-back rooms abounds with storage ideas that satisfy the entire family.

The trick to packing in kid-tough, adult-savvy storage in this flowing country-modern gathering space came down to carefully considering the purpose of each area and then incorporating as many multipurpose items as possible.

In the living room area, the built-in fireplace surround provides architectural focus and a multitude of storage opportunities. The mantel creates the perfect perch for artwork or off-duty serving pieces, while the shelving nooks offer versatile display and storage for media equipment, art, games, and books. A slipcovered storage ottoman works quadruple duty as a sitting place, footrest, tray table, and toy box. Once on-call in a school cafeteria, the metal cart enjoys a second life as a mobile drink and snack station. The homeowners can stock it in the kitchen, use it to serve in the family room, and then roll it back to the kitchen to dispose of dirty dishes and trash.

Unconventional yet super-functional additions are essential in the family work area. Here, a basic plywood table is topped with simple, versatile storage items, such as a letter, tray, bowl, and lazy Susan and surrounded by easy-to-reposition stools. In the media area, no-fuss, flexible storage makes the space comfortable and organized. Sleek wall ledges hold up an assorted collection of artwork and family photos, while distressed wood furniture—which actually looks better with daily wear and tear—supports the TV set and organizes media materials.

THIS PHOTO: A distressed chest in the media area stands in for an end table (and holds a bevy of games and gear), while the television rests on a flea market table. OPPOSITE: Wood ledges make mixing and matching art easy.

For storage that's family-friendly and stylish, choose **finishes** and fabrics that are already **distressed** and thoroughly scrubbable.

● **Original built-ins** that flank the fireplace, *opposite,* were updated with paint and beaded-board backing. Beautiful boxes and baskets fill the bottom shelves. ● **A salvaged metal cart,** *left,* has all the right moves as an entertainment station overflowing with snacks, drinks, napkins, and more. ● **A square lampshade** and oversize paper clips, *above left,* become an instant memo board for photos and notes, while a vintage lazy Susan serves up office supplies. ● **Three bright red stools,** *above right,* are easy to move around the room thanks to holes drilled in the seats.

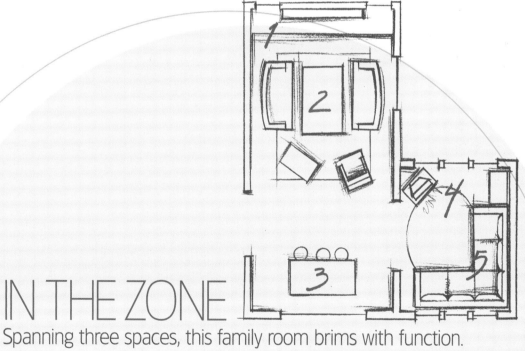

IN THE ZONE
Spanning three spaces, this family room brims with function.

1 store
After removing cabinet doors, the resulting open shelves offer easy access to books, photo albums, and a stereo system.

2 play
By outfitting the coffee table and storage ottoman with wheels, the pieces provide flexible seating, footrests, and places for trays.

3 work
The custom work table and stools are light enough to move around the area, accommodating evening homework or whole-family projects.

4 watch
Instead of a bulky entertainment center, a weathered farm table houses the television. Baskets below hold DVDs and a game system.

5 display
Ledges display an ever-changing collection of photos and art. The family stores undisplayed pieces under the skirted sectional.

smart solutions
media storage

Use flexible arrangements that keep up with ever-evolving home electronics.

1 ANGLING FOR VIEWS Hide the heavy-duty mounting gear for a flat-panel television between wall studs. Mask the unit's shallow depth with doors and drawers that mimic the look of a classic built-in.

2 ON A ROLL Wheeled garage cabinets slip under a wall-mounted television, giving the appearance of a cohesive entertainment center.

3 LONG AND LOW Line a wall with 18- to 20-inch-tall cabinets; top with bookcase units and pillows as needed to outfit the space as the size and shape of media changes.

4 BUILT FOR OPENNESS For visual continuity, a television and stacked media bins wrap around a corner and connect to dining room cabinetry beyond.

if you only have one hour...

Untangle all those cords behind your media center. Bundle excess cord with repositionable ties (look for ones made of hook-and-loop tape). At the outlet or power strip, label every cord with a tag or sticker.

smart solutions
bookcases

Make these classic storage pieces work even harder with clever adaptations.

1 COOL CORNERS Slim bookcases give function to an underused corner, but the real beauty of this open design is that each shelf turns 90 degrees, eliminating a central divider.

2 SHALLOW SPLENDOR Just 4 inches deep, this bookcase organizes children's books or magazines behind nautical-themed decorative trim and rope.

3 CLOSET CLUSTER Line an entire wall with ready-to-assemble closet components—including shoe organizers and drawer units—to mimic the look of a custom built-in.

4 FRAME JOB Open and bin-style cabinets claim the once-wasted space around and above a piano flanked by French doors.

smart solutions
bench seating

Stow stuff and kick back in comfort with these double-duty additions.

3

2

4

1 UP, OVER & UNDER Flanked by bookcases and topped with open shelving, a cozy daybed nook provides display space for collections and books, as well as hideaway storage for blankets and electronics.

2 CLEVER CONVERSION Two semicustom kitchen cabinets are topped with solid-surfacing and function as a window seat. Outfitted with a cushion, the spot is ideal for slipping on shoes or stashing seasonal gear.

3 TABLE SERVICE Pillows and a long wicker basket give an old coffee table new purpose. Small drawers can be dedicated to just one type of item, such as CDs or card games.

4 GRAB AND GO Wrapping a hinge-top box with wainscoting and hooks transforms a forgotten area into a mini mudroom.

⏱ if you only have one hour...
Replace a coffee or end table with an upholstered storage cube. Available for less than $40 at discount stores, these hardworking pieces store books or toys and can be instantly called into service as seating.

smart solutions
china hutches

Display your dishes and set the table quickly with these do-it-yourself cabinets.

2

1 POSTER POWER Black-and-white images dry-mounted on pieces of presentation board function as backs for three open shelving units. Hanging the boards on alternating sides dramatically divides the room and offers storage space for serving pieces in the dining area and collections in the living area.

2 PAINTED PRESENCE Adjustable metal wall shelving takes on the look of a substantial furniture piece when mounted atop two bold bands of wall paint.

3 MIX AND MATCH Half of a salvaged bedroom dresser serves as the upper portion of a china hutch. A rustic farm table (outfitted with casters so it can be moved easily around the room) holds entertaining essentials.

3

smart solutions
party central

Let the good times flow with these clever entertainment stations.

1 FULL-SERVICE SOLUTION Fill a niche with built-ins and include beverage-related appliances such as a refrigerator and wine cooler. Display drinkware in glass-front upper cabinets and hide a blender, juicer, and hand mixer in closed lower units.

2 COOL RETOOL Convert a vintage icebox into a self-contained bar. Remove refrigeration elements and spray-paint the exterior. (Consider having the hardware professionally cleaned or refinished.)

3 BUREAU BAR Remove drawers from a dresser, then line the spaces and fashion wine dividers from the salvaged wood.

4 FOLD-UP FUN Transform a corner into an impromptu spot for drinks by topping a luggage rack with a lipped serving tray.

smart solutions on display

Squeeze in surprising spots to show off some of your favorite things.

1 IN A HALLWAY Long strips of metal edging mounted to one wall serve as an ever-changing art gallery. A slim, low credenza anchors the display and provides additional storage.

2 IN A CORNER A slender tower-style unit capitalizes on the 18×18-inch patch of floor space frequently found near the passageway between rooms.

3 BETWEEN SPACES Open shelves reach from floor to ceiling, creating an entry area and offering two-sided displays, which are ideal for glass and pottery collections.

4 ON THE WALL A grid of painted 2×4s atop grass-cloth wallpaper creates shallow display ledges that echo the look of wall studs.

high and low Make the most of space above and below windows. Add a 1×4 board to the top of a window frame to create a ledge for dishes. Combine crates and storage cubes to fill the 18 to 24 inches of space typically found below a window.

12 fast fixes: entertainment center

Have your favorite fun-time activities at your fingertips with an entertainment armoire.

solutions:

1 Select a cabinet with adjustable shelves to accommodate equipment and media.

2 Shrink the size of your home stereo system with an mp3 player and speakers station.

3 Gather accessories for digital cameras in shallow baskets or bins.

4 Stand CDs in racks that allow you to flip through your collection.

5 Categorize DVDs by genre with labeled wicker baskets.

6 Sort and display photos in customizable photo albums.

7 Drop disposable media, such as newspapers and TV guides, in a portable basket.

8 Display magazines in a wire rack as if they were books.

9 Look for an armoire with drawers of varying depth to store electronics and media.

10 Mount a wood bin inside the cabinet door to hold remotes and accessories.

11 Incorporate divided bins into a game drawer to keep small pieces and cards in place.

12 Quickly plug in or recharge electronics with a grounded power strip installed in the cabinet's back.

bedroom
spaces

GETTING A GOOD NIGHT'S SLEEP IS EASIER WHEN YOUR BEDROOM IS FREE FROM DISTRACTIONS. RELY ON THE SOLUTIONS IN THIS CHAPTER TO SERENELY STORE MORE IN YOUR SLEEP SPACE. SWEET DREAMS . . .

buttoned-up
master suite

A remodeled sleep space offers a bevy of built-ins for stashing and stowing.

Every inch of available space in this redesigned master suite is devoted to efficient—and unexpected—storage ideas. Before the remodel, two tiny closets provided the only real storage. Now, vintage-look built-ins wrap the entire room. With its all-white paint treatment, the handsome cabinetry unifies the space and more than triples the room's original storage capacity. Doors and drawers in various shapes and orientations make getting dressed a cinch with appropriately sized areas for hanging and storing clothes, lingerie, sweaters, and accessories.

Even the room's focal-point bed is a storage-rich built-in. Its base features deep drawers to tuck away extra bedding or off-season clothes; the slanted headboard creates a shelf for clocks and a slim stereo; and a hidden armrest can be pulled down for comfortable reading. Built-in dressers on either side of the bed double as nightstands and are topped with tower-style bookshelves—one unit even has a drawer that pulls out to act as a bedside table, while the other has a drawer custom-built to house and charge a laptop.

The built-in theme continues in the bathroom. Replacing a lone little vanity, the new double-sink unit has lots of drawers to tuck away toiletries. The biggest benefit of all these built-ins? The ability to shut the door or drawer on any clutter so the rooms always feel clean, crisp, and organized.

THIS PHOTO: File this idea under "useful": a bed base that has deep drawers to stash items you don't need often. OPPOSITE: A sliding lid turns a bedside drawer into a handy table.

Built-ins close off clutter, and using the same neutral color scheme for all units presents a soothing, unified front.

● **The furniturelike feel of built-ins** topped with marble surfaces and accented with elegant hardware, *opposite,* make the suite feel like an architecturally complete room, not just a collection of storage units. ● **An inexpensive tray insert** converts a drawer, *left,* into slotted jewelry storage. Adding simple cup hooks on the walls of a cedar-lined cubby organizes necklaces. ● **Bench seats,** *above left,* tuck into two corners of the bedroom, hiding radiators and introducing extra book storage. ● **A sleek double-sink vanity,** *above right,* maximizes storage in the small master bath.

IN THE ZONE

Wrapped with built-ins, this master suite has room for every amenity.

1 prep
A double-sink vanity with multiple drawers tucks away sundries such as makeup and towels, while a pair of medicine cabinets keeps small essentials close at hand.

2 unwind
Two banks of window seats make clever covers for radiators, introduce extra book storage, and give the room multiple spots for reading or enjoying the views.

3 organize
A centrally located bank of built-ins resembles two chests and a dresser, but it hugs the wall more tightly than individual pieces, freeing up valuable floor space.

4 rest
Surrounding the bed with shelves means necessities—a stereo, clock, books, and more—are always within reach. One drawer converts to a mini bedside table.

5 stash
Drawers in the bed's base reclaim unused space and are perfect for stashing extra bedding or seasonal clothing. Office-inspired labels allow for flexibility.

squeeze in
more storage

Elegant style and efficient storage partner perfectly in this bed and bath.

Storage-rich is an adjective you might not associate with ranch-style homes. But when the owners of this beloved rambler in suburban Chicago decided to reconfigure and extend an awkward 14-year-old bedroom addition, all their choices hinged on ways to stylishly integrate closets, cabinetry, and other storage staples into the space. The result is a beautiful mix of urban chic and gracious charm, as well as a seamless blend of lush artisanship and hardworking organization.

Proximity to a neighboring house gave the new bedroom a long windowless wall—a natural place to include matching walk-in closets. To ensure this wall of storage would feel distinctive and make the most of limited natural light, it was lined with eight mirrored doors. Two doors access the closets, while the other six open to 12-inch-deep shelves ideal for books, shoes, and folded clothes.

On the other side of the suite's fireplace, the revamped master bath feels like it's been cultivated over time. Mirror-front cabinets and vintage-style built-ins wrap the room. Skirted vanities that resemble converted farm tables are connected by a lower dressing station, which accommodates an existing window and infuses the room with unfitted charm.

THIS PHOTO: A wall of reclaimed brick functions as a secondary storage headboard. OPPOSITE: A built-in resembling a Shaker-style armoire fills a nook between the fireplace and a wall of mirror-fronted storage.

● **New built-ins with mirrored doors** arranged in pairs, *opposite,* double the bathroom's apparent size and look like vintage hutches. ● **A linen-skirted vanity,** *left,* hides laundry baskets and trash bins while softening the room's rugged brick walls.
● **A storage cubby and medicine cabinet** beside each sink, *above left,* provide a spot for individual storage of grooming essentials.
● **The new powder room,** *above right,* opens into both the main hallway and master bath, so the homeowners or guests can access it.

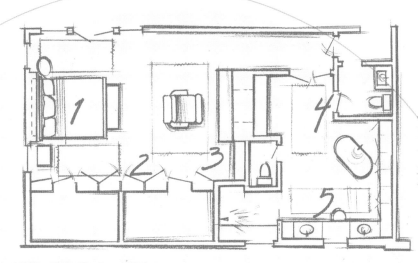

IN THE ZONE
Clever architecture masks abundant storage in this sophisticated suite.

1 display
A shallow 1×7-foot niche showcases favorite pottery and books. The wall also functions as an architectural headboard for the king-size bed.

2 dress
Eight doors lead to two walk-in closets and six storage cases. Mirror fronts widen the long room and capitalize on natural light from transom-topped French doors.

3 relax
A leather recliner cozies up to the open fireplace and flat-panel TV, while a nearby built-in armoire holds DVDs, stereo equipment, and snacks.

4 prep
With the flip of a lock, the new secondary bathroom can be utilized by guests as a powder room or by the homeowners as an additional spot to get ready.

5 primp
A pair of skirted vanities look like antique furniture but function like individual grooming stations thanks to personal storage cubbies and medicine cabinets.

clear up
kid clutter

Small-space solutions yield a child's room that creatively manages chaos.

Space planning was the greatest challenge in transforming this second-floor space into a little girl's dream bedroom. The room brimmed with vintage Craftsman-style, but that didn't necessarily mean good organization. Ultimately, working with the room's limited square footage and angled ceilings proved to be the project's greatest reward, forcing space to be used as efficiently as possible. The biggest goal was to offer plenty of open floor for play without a bed jutting out into the middle of the room. To that end, a twin bed was custom-built to tuck under a bank of windows. Cabinets (ordered from a home center and sold as kitchen storage) flank the bed, while a large drawer beneath gives plenty of space to stow clothes and toys. At some point in the future, this drawer can be converted into a trundle bed for sleepover guests.

The room's storage high point grew from an inauspicious closet with odd angles. After widening the doorway, bifold French doors were added to make it a true walk-in. The closet also calls into service an often overlooked area: excess dormer space. After knocking out a section of wall, adding insulation, and installing cabinets, this once-wasted space now earns its keep. The closet also does more than organize clothing thanks to the addition of a window seat, cute curtains, and cozy carpet tiles. The space is now the perfect secret hideaway to read a book or write in a journal.

THIS PHOTO: An upholstered window seat offers a quiet spot to perch in the closet, while parallel clothes rods double the hanging potential for clothes. OPPOSITE: An accordion-style coat rack makes the most of a sliver of wall space under the eaves.

Encourage storage and organization as part of a child's daily routine by rewarding a week's worth of clutter-free floors, put-away toys, or well-made beds.

● **Basic home-center cabinets,** *opposite top,* are embellished with blue ceramic knobs and surround the twin bed as built-in dressers. ● **A cabinet designed for office supplies,** *opposite below,* hides a child's little treasures. ● **Color-coded fabric-covered boxes** with labels, *left,* encourage young ones to learn organization. ● **Floating shelves with buckets** in the pint-size kitchen space, *above,* invite sorting games, while the appliances themselves offer ample storage space for dishes and other toys. ● **A wide underbed drawer,** *above right,* holds toys now but can be outfitted with a mattress for sleepovers.

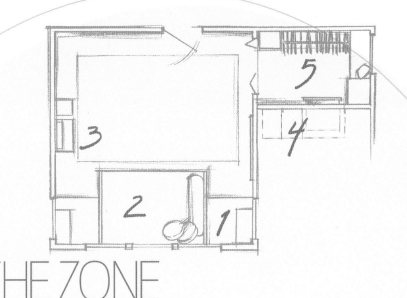

IN THE ZONE
Home-center cabinets pump up the storage in this bedroom.

1 open up
Placing built-in cabinets and the bed parallel to the wall opens up the center of the room for a portable play table and stools.

2 sleep
A twin bed tops a large drawer that can be filled with toys or blankets—or outfitted with an additional mattress to function as a trundle bed.

3 play
Open shelves, color-coded buckets, clear containers, and a combination peg board/bulletin board introduce kids to organization.

4 stash
Filling the angled, undereaves space with a trio of built-in drawers claims forgotten cubic feet for even more clothing storage.

5 hang out
Double-hung rods hold tons of clothing, while a new window seat offers a space to dress in the morning or just kick back with a book.

secrets of
sharing a closet

Hardworking components maximize limited space in this storage suite.

Talk about a thing of beauty: an intelligently designed and well-organized closet that makes the most of every available square inch for an economical price. With only standard storage components, this thoroughly basic walk-in closet—8×10 feet, with one door and an inefficient wraparound hanging bar and a shelf for clothes—was transformed into a fully outfitted partner closet and miniature dressing room.

First, the homeowners ruthlessly edited their wardrobes and then calculated the number of pants, shirts, suits, dresses, shoes, and accessories they needed to store. With the free assistance of a design consultant, they figured out the number of rods, drawers, and shelves they needed, allowing flexibility for each clothing category to grow up to 15 percent. Removing a few shelves and inserting drawer dividers further customized the ready-to-assemble storage components.

The consultant also helped incorporate specialty components for housing laundry, linens, out-of-season garments, and laundry-prep tools. With the final touches of upgraded overhead lighting, a slim dressing bench, and a custom-cut mirror, the revamped closet sizzles with style and function.

THIS PHOTO: His side of the closet allots space for towels, pillows, and a three-section laundry hamper on wheels. OPPOSITE: Canvas inserts optimize organization inside a large drawer.

● **Garment-specific hangers** on her side of the closet, *opposite,* organize an array of fashions, while boxes and bins gather smaller items. ● **The space created by removing a few shelves,** *left,* functions as a dressing station. A small mirror, framed photos, perfume bottles, and a jewelry box personalize the niche. ● **A side-mount rack,** *above left,* keeps neckties neat, accessible, and wrinkle-free. A matching rack below (not shown) organizes belts. ● **A canvas box filled with laundry accessories,** *above right,* encourages on-the-fly clothing fixes.

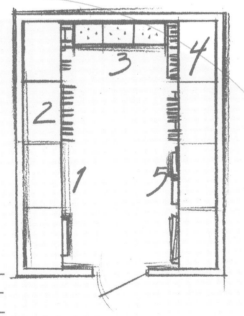

IN THE ZONE
Wrapping a small room in storage components yields big results.

1 sort
Four large drawers are dedicated to housing only hosiery, lingerie, and accessories. Plastic dividers and canvas boxes bring order to these vast spaces.

2 stack
Shirts hang from the upper bar, while pants and skirts are hung below. A shelf between the two introduces the perfect 10-inch-tall spot for stashing hats.

3 dress
A cushioned bench with cubbies can hold a dozen pairs of shoes in acrylic boxes. Backed by a custom-cut 4×5-foot mirror, the area functions as a cozy dressing room.

4 clean
A three-bin hamper tucks into the extra space under a hanging bar for pants. The cart can be rolled out for doing laundry and returned with fresh clothes.

5 store
Canvas boxes with cedar inserts protect off-season clothing on upper shelves. Extra bed linens and towels stack near the closet's entrance for quick access.

1

smart solutions
bedside storage

Design the area around your bed to offer both function and style.

1 HEADBOARD HERO A thick headboard (this one is nearly 12 inches deep) offers a generous top display ledge and side cubbies ideal for favorite books and bedside essentials.

2 UP AND AROUND Covering the wall space beside and above a bed with shallow custom or stock cabinets (the upper cabinet doors are removed) capitalizes on underused space.

3 PILE IT UP Fill the abundant cubic feet under a lofted bed with a cabinet and drawers on extending rails. The bottom drawer contains a trundle bed.

4 REACH HIGH AND WIDE A wall of bookcases functions as a massive headboard and houses abundant books and collections. Personal items are discreetly stored in boxes.

trundle trick Beds with space for an extra pullout mattress are available in numerous styles and price points. Rather than filling the trundle pullout with a mattress, use the space as a large-scale drawer and store extra bedding, toys, or off-season clothing.

smart solutions
nightstands

Pack in the storage with these unconventional bedside tables.

1 FROM THE OFFICE Mobile office furniture is durable, flexible, and sophisticated —perfect for introducing sleek storage into a streamlined bedroom. A file cabinet can double as an occasional table, while a printer stand houses electronics and reading material.

2 FROM THE LIVING ROOM Stack a storage cube and reading lamp atop a similarly finished coffee table to instantly create a piece of custom bedside furniture.

3 FROM THE PANTRY Refinish a basic wooden vegetable bin and use it as a nightstand with casual cubbies perfectly sized to hold toys, clothes, and bedtime reading material.

smart solutions
bedroom built-ins

Line the walls of your sleep space with functional cabinets and shelving.

1 ANGLED ORGANIZATION Outfit the interior of a closet (or a wall section that bumps out approximately 18 inches) with a grid of diagonally oriented bookshelves. Fill the cubbies with books, memorabilia, rolled-up clothing, throws, or extra bedding.

2 WINDOW SURROUND Shallow bookcases with adjustable shelves wrap around and above a small window, converting the wall into an expansive storage system. Two slim mattresses atop four low drawer units serve as a daybed for reading or hosting overnight guests.

3 BUMP-OUT MEDIA A custom-built entertainment center surrounds an old chimney flue, boasting doored cabinets on the front and open shelving on either side. A pair of inviting window seats extends from the unit.

1

smart solutions
closets
Include these handy features, and getting dressed can be a dream.

1 CENTRAL STATION A slim dressing island provides spots for partners to lay out the day's outfits. Reed baskets accessible from either side of open cubbies organize a bevy of final flourishes.

2 IN THE SWING A swiveling rack makes the most of a closet's often-forgotten sidewall. Ten wooden rods display trousers and can be pushed aside for compact storage.

3 NIFTY TOPPER A 6-inch-tall glass shelf doubles the limited counter space on a storage peninsula and allows you to safely set out accessories and jewelry.

4 STYLISH SLIDE-OUTS A gliding tray for belts and ties and a hamper unit replace basic, stationary shelves in the lower portion of a built-in cabinet unit.

dirty laundry Include ample room in your closet storage plans for clothing to be washed. One bin is rarely enough—even for a single person—so choose a container, measure it, then double the needed floor space and also add a few inches of vertical space.

smart solutions
clothing

Dressing for success is a breeze with these fashionable organizers.

2

3

1 STAGING STATION Designate an occasional table as a spot for the next day's outfit. Small suitcases of accessories make finding finishing touches a breeze. If floor space is limited, consider a small wheeled kitchen cart that you can roll into service when needed.

2 EASY ACCESS In a kid's closet, opt for repositionable wire components. Low shelves and a stack of slide-out drawers can be replaced by more hanging storage as a child grows.

3 BAR BASICS Use the same hanger in different colors to designate clothing based on season or type. Plastic retail tags labeled with dry-erase marker provide an additional layer of organization, while metal S-hooks allow bags and purses to hang face-forward.

smart solutions
accessories

An organized closet includes storage for a world of wardrobe essentials.

1 FOR SHOES Clear vinyl shoe bags hang on a door in minutes and can be quickly cut with scissors to fit your closet's dimensions. (Shoebags are also a great way to store rolled up belts, gloves, purses, and other accessories.)

2 FOR SOCKS Clear acrylic trays designed to organize office supplies or kitchen utensils can bring beautiful order to your hosiery drawer.

3 FOR JEWELRY Fill the compartments of several small art-supply trays with necklaces, bracelets, rings, and more.

4 FOR EVERYTHING ELSE Purchase lidded cardboard boxes in various sizes and shapes and fill them with clusters of similar accessories. Affix removable labels so you know each box's contents.

now you see it Choose clear storage containers. Being able to see into boxes from any angle improves your chances of finding what you're looking for. If clear containers aren't possible, create accurate labels that are easy to update.

14 fast fixes: can-do closet

Convert an extra bedroom closet into a spot for pursuing favorite creative activities.

solutions:

1. Collect and categorize fabric scraps in small laundry baskets.

2. Attach cardboard tags to spiral-coil key chains to label overhead containers.

3. Fill handled baskets with project-specific supplies and hang from cup hooks.

4. Repurpose wall-mount plate racks to hold files, magazines, and mail.

5. Drop notes, clippings, and receipts into color-coded accordion files.

6. Stack mini plastic crates to create tower-style storage units.

7. Line the back of the closet with cork and magnetic boards to showcase bits of inspiration.

8. Install an 18-inch-deep shelf 30 inches from the floor to serve as a desk.

9. Stand rolls of kraft and wrapping paper in a wastebasket.

10. Use a paper towel holder to display spools of ribbon.

11. Slip tools into pouches made from folded dish towels.

12. Drape cards and envelopes over the slats of a wire baking rack.

13. Load metal wall vases with colored pencils and paintbrushes.

14. Replace the ID forms inside luggage tags with decorative paper for fun, flexible labels.

bath
spaces

WHEN YOU'RE ON THE GO, AN ORGANIZED BATH IS A HASSLE-FREE ZONE IN WHICH YOU CAN PREPARE FOR A BUSY DAY OR PRIMP FOR AN EVENING OUT. BANISH CLUTTER FROM YOUR BATH SPACE WITH THE IDEAS IN THIS CHAPTER.

clean and
clutter-free

Efficient design makes use of every inch of space with a bounty of versatile storage.

A complete remodel of this master bathroom retained the original footprint and fixture placement but improved its function by adding a multitude of storage options to the 12×20-foot space. The custom, cottage-style pieces visually relate to one another but have distinct functions. Along one long wall, an arched, paneled surround highlights the vanity area, which includes double sinks and a versatile combination of drawers, upper and lower cabinets, and shelves that hold clutter, including towels, hair dryers, and cosmetics.

A new whirlpool tub sits at a jaunty angle opposite a corner window seat, which offers a cushioned lounge area above under-the-seat storage drawers. In between these two features, a floor-to-ceiling storage tower adds a practical bevy of drawers, shelves, and cabinet space, as well as furniturelike appeal and architectural detail. Glass doors lighten up the unit and introduce display space. A space-efficient built-in armoire replaces a linen closet at the end of the short hallway to the master bedroom, offering more customized organization and a lighted, arched display nook.

Every effort was made to coax out as much storage as possible in the room. A tiny cabinet tucks in next to the tub, and a shallow band of molding atop the beaded-board paneling displays candles and starfish. There is even a flat-screen TV in this storage-rich space, cleverly hidden behind cabinet doors in the storage tower near the tub.

THIS PHOTO: A corner window seat is a clever and comfortable way to combine seating and deep drawer storage in the limited space under the windows. OPPOSITE: A 3-inch deep ledge finishes off the beaded-board paneling and provides display space that wraps around the room.

● **Hooks on one wall** of the shower enclosure, *right,* offer spots for hanging up towels and robes. A small table with a bowl of washcloths anchors the arrangement. ● **Glass-front cabinets** and bin-style drawers, *below,* are furniturelike details that boost the cabinetry's function. ● **An expansive double vanity area,** *far right,* houses medicine and toiletries in upper flanking cabinets, towels in open shelves, and bath essentials in deep lower drawers.

Although adorned with vintage details, this bath's hard-working built-ins are designed for modern living.

● **A corner whirlpool tub,** *opposite,* seems less intrusive when angled beneath a window and surrounded by a wide, tile-covered ledge. ● **Crystal barware containers,** *left,* give everyday toiletries sophisticated style. ● **Tall cabinets** on either end of the double vanity, *above left,* open from two sides for easy access to everyday items such as toothbrushes, cotton swabs, and lotions. ● **A custom armoire,** *above right,* replaces the original linen closet at the end of the hallway to the master bedroom, introducing architectural interest and even more options for storage and display.

IN THE ZONE

Brimming with built-ins, this bath has room for every amenity.

1 prep
Getting ready is a breeze thanks to the vanity's two sinks, open shelves, pair of tall toiletry cabinets, and expansive undercounter drawers.

2 soak
A corner tub's tiled ledge provides a comfortable seat and keeps bath supplies, candles, and towels within easy reach while bathing.

3 stash
A storage tower corrals clutter. Glass-front cabinets keep the look light and showcase pretty accessories; six bins impart vintage-inspired style.

4 relax
An upholstered window seat holds books, blankets, and extra towels in broad drawers. Plus, the spot affords restful backyard views.

5 dress
The built-in armoire between the master bedroom and bath houses fresh linens, a hamper, and clothing items, such as pajamas and underwear.

streamlined
organization

Minimal design requires planning for maximum storage as this retreat proves.

A bathroom that looks (and stays!) uncluttered must have strategically designed storage to capture the items that accumulate in this high-use area. This remodeled master bath clearly accomplishes the goal of streamlined storage, thanks to custom cabinets, rotating vanity mirrors, and built-in organizers.

The room's high, round window inspired the softly bowing cherry cabinetry below it. A stack of four drawers between the two vessel sinks provides the ideal place for shared bathroom items. To the left of the sinks, a makeup area features a vertical cabinet for discreetly drying wet towels as well as columns of drawers and a place to stow a chair. The layout enables the homeowners to tuck everything from face cream to hairspray to necklaces neatly out of sight. Across from the vanity, an armoire-style storage unit has dimensions generous enough to hold towels, bathrobes, bath mats, and even a pair of laundry basket.

The clean-lined look continues above the sinks with five frameless mirrors. When pivoted on their brackets, the mirrors reveal multiple shelves. These lipped trays make ideal perches for toothpaste, lotions, and the other items that commonly inhabit medicine cabinets. In the nearby shower, shallow nooks recessed into the French Fontenay Claire limestone walls house soap, sponges, bottles, and brushes. Floating conveniently above the tub, a dual-purpose towel rack—inspired by hotel-style storage—holds fresh folded linens above and wet towels below.

THIS PHOTO: Two bow-front vanities add a few extra square feet of storage space in the balanced sink area. OPPOSITE: Mirrors with hidden storage compensate for the bath's streamlined countertops and vessel sinks.

Built-in cabinets, shower nooks, and hidden towel racks keep this space clutter-free and reinforce the room's sleek and modern vibe.

• **Built-in shower nooks,** *opposite,* wide tub ledges, and a wall-mount towel rack provide sunny spots for supplies and towels.
• **A dressing table,** *left,* was created by removing a wall and extending the sink area countertop. • **A skinny pullout section** between the sink and dressing table, *above left,* was inspired by a similar feature in the homeowners' kitchen. Fitted with metal bars, the cabinet stows damp hand towels. • **Above-the-sink mirrors,** *above right,* pivot to reveal shelving and function as nontraditional medicine cabinets. Metal lips and rubber liners ensure items stay in place.

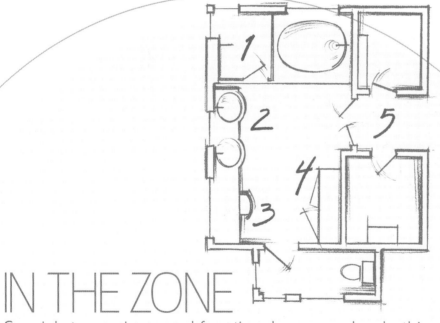

IN THE ZONE
Special storage in several functional areas makes bathing serene.

1 bathe
Thick ledges around the whirlpool tub and built-in limestone niches in the shower function as resting spots for towels and toiletries.

2 prep
Twin vessel sinks allow two people to get ready efficiently. Five pivoting vanity mirrors hide grooming supplies.

3 primp
The top drawer on the built-in dressing table area works as a single rolling tray, which is ideal for holding makeup and jewelry.

4 store
A built-in armoire organizes an abundance of bath linens and robes. A rod and hooks let bathers hang up today's outfit.

5 dress
French doors between the bath and two walk-in closets can be adjusted for privacy or free-flowing connection.

1

smart solutions vanities

A great bath begins with a sink or two surrounded by splash-friendly storage.

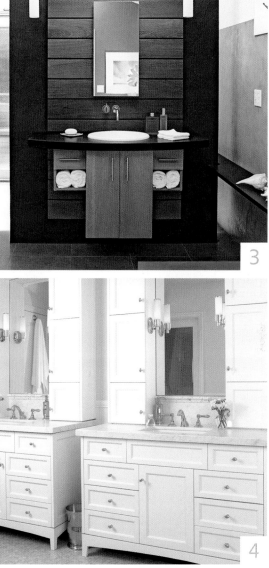

1 BACKING ACTION Complement an open-style vanity with integrated wall storage. This newly constructed bath wall provides a 9-inch-deep recess for three open display niches and a pair of medicine cabinets.

2 PEDESTAL PLUS Placing a sculptural sink in front of shallow built-ins yields an airy, sophisticated look that still accommodates lots of grooming supplies.

3 CUBBY CONNECTION Gain function by including open areas in cabinets. Open storage is ideal for towels, hair dryers, and other grab-and-go items.

4 HIGH-MINDED Flank a mirror with tall, narrow cabinets for a furniture-style vanity that lets you keep toiletries nearby yet hidden.

if you only have one hour...

Make over a vanity drawer by emptying and then thoroughly cleaning it. Toss everything that's expired—no exceptions! Line with wipeable paper and divide the space with spring-loaded panels and acrylic trays.

smart solutions
toiletries

Grab grooming essentials and little luxuries in seconds with these add-ons.

1 DOORS WITH MORE Shallow wood-and-wire racks mounted inside cabinet doors claim unused space for bath-time goodies.

2 NO-SLIP SLOTS Using furniture tacks, attach lace, elastic, or ribbon to drawer interiors to create a series of compartments sized to fit your beauty supplies.

3 SPINNING STYLE Boost the function of a deep linen cabinet with a lazy Susan that holds bottles, clear canisters, and open containers for brushes and tall, skinny items.

4 STREAMLINED & SPICY A slim pullout cabinet, inspired by kitchen spice storage, organizes an array of odd-size bath products behind a single smooth-gliding door.

if you only have one hour...
Shop an office supply store—for bath storage. Plastic desk caddies function well as makeup organizers, wall-mount file bins are great inside of cabinets, and mail holders can arrange a week's worth of washcloths.

smart solutions
towel bars

Repurposed items and creative placement update this classic bathroom element.

1 RUNG UP Think high rather than wide when you call an old ladder into storage service. Repainted with a gloss finish, this piece is ideal in a bath for guests or kids because everyone can have a spot.

2 RACK SOLID A wall-mount hotel shelf puts towels, washcloths, and robes within easy reach of a bathtub or shower.

3 PASSING THE BAR Drape linens and relaxing reading material over a vintage staircase railing that extends the length of a soaking tub.

4 OUTSIDE THE BOX Towel bars and rings mount to bath cabinet exteriors as easily as walls. Add these features to the cabinet sides and fronts, just below the countertop. For a streamlined look, forgo knobs and handles on doors outfitted with towel bars.

1

smart solutions
bath helpers

Freestanding pieces add welcome flexibility for storing bath essentials.

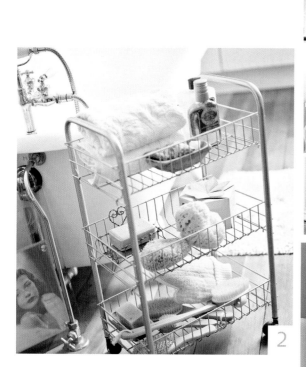

1 CENTER OF ATTENTION An old-fashioned pharmacy cabinet professionally spray-painted fresh green pairs a glass-front upper portion for displaying collectibles with practical closed storage below for discreetly hiding toiletries.

2 CONVENIENT CART A metal cart keeps bath-time supplies nearby whenever you need them—and rolled away when you don't.

3 ARMOIRE STYLE An antique French bookcase moves out of the library and into the bath to offer sophisticated storage space for towels, soaps, and other essentials.

4 INTEGRATED DESIGN Visually connect freestanding cabinets and give them a built-in look by installing molding between units.

smart vanities Pedestal and console sinks offer a sophisticated look, but they limit storage space. To ensure you'll have room for your toothbrush and other necessities, choose a model with plenty of counter space or an integrated shelf below the sink.

smart solutions
linen closets

Provide stylish quarters for your freshly laundered towels and sheets.

1 COMPACT CLOSET Baskets corral similar items in this well-organized closet. To fit more linens into the limited area, comforters are rolled and tied with ribbon. A hamper keeps dirty clothes neatly tucked out of sight, while a pair of towel bars puts the back of the door to work.

2 CORNER CABINET A small corner is home to a stylish built-in linen cabinet. Louvered doors and vintage glass knobs on the compact unit bring cottage appeal to a simple design.

3 WALL WRAPPERS Four long shelves and a wide-drawer dresser offer plenty of organization. Vinyl letters charmingly identify drawer contents, while lipped shelves keep stacks of towels in place.

smart solutions in the shower

Keep your bathing gear organized in this small sliver of space.

1 ON DISPLAY Frosted-glass shelves are cleverly tucked into a dry spot within a partial wall of this walk-in shower.

2 NEAT NOOKS Twin tiled niches carved out between wall studs offer easily accessible storage and spots for shelves and racks attached with suction cups.

3 BENCH WARMER Built-in benches provide a convenient seat in the shower, but they also can double as a handy landing place for grooming supplies.

4 STREAMLINED STYLE Clean up bottles of shampoo, conditioner, and body wash—and upgrade the look of your shower area—with stylish dispensers that hang on the wall.

in the corner Make the most of small shower stalls by installing storage units that tuck into a corner, adding function without getting in the way. Look for triangular shelves, baskets that mount on a central pole, and mesh bags.

12 fast fixes: bathroom vanity

Beat the morning rush when you upgrade your primping zone with these simple additions.

solutions:

1 Fill a toothpick dispenser with cotton swabs.

2 Organize toiletries for specific task, such as manicures, in vinyl travel bags.

3 Arrange nail polish in a plastic tray with an angled bottom.

4 Display everyday essentials in a plastic tray that you can whisk away when company arrives.

5 Slip hot hair care tools into wall-mount holsters.

6 Hang hair care products on a rack of hooks designed for keys.

7 Replace vanity doors with double swing rods; one rod holds a privacy curtain, the other, hand towels.

8 Round up less frequently used tools and products in canvas baskets under the counter.

9 Inside baskets, affix elastic bands (with a few dots of fabric glue) to keep bottles from tumbling.

10 Organize cavernous undervanity space with a sliding rack; look for side- or bottom-mount systems.

11 Fill handled pails with frequently accessed beauty accessories.

12 Tuck jewelry in the compartments of a ceramic egg tray.

TO DO:

8 a.m. Advisor club

Noon Swim

1:30 Meet Sabrina
2:30

Pick up
Staples, paper,
tape, printer ink
Hp 57

Markers

1

2

3

Pencils

work
spaces

TO COMPLETE A PROJECT OR DO A LOAD OF LAUNDRY, YOU NEED AREAS WHERE YOU CAN SPREAD OUT. THE IDEAS IN THIS CHAPTER WILL HELP YOU CARVE OUT FUNCTIONAL, GOOD-LOOKING SPACES TO GET THING DONE.

small space,
many purposes

This tiny bonus room is the hardest working space in the house.

Highly underused, depressingly dark, and decidedly unfunctional, this hodgepodge den required major rethinking to meet the needs of a young family. First, the family needed a basic work space—but having somewhere to stash mounds of toys and welcome a guest for the night were on the wish list too. That's a tall order for a 13×14-foot room, but careful planning and creative design helped accomplish their vision.

Lining two entire walls with pearly-white cabinetry in place of the original dark bookcases instantly brightened the room. With two desks, everyone has a zone in which to play and work—and parents' paperwork is kept far from the finger paints. Parents claim upper cabinets, and kids' items fill lower ones so they can reach toys and games as well as put them away when it's time to clean up.

The varying cabinet sizes and styles were chosen to accommodate the range of items that call this room home. Listing and measuring items to store before you begin helps determine cabinet type as well as placement. A double-door cabinet, for instance, was selected to house a large dollhouse. Increasing the depth of some wall cabinets from the standard 12 inches to 15 inches made a remarkable difference in how they function. Outfitting cabinet interiors with carefully chosen drawer organizers and storage bins makes them work even smarter.

THIS PHOTO: With a smart and playful layout, kitchen cabinets ordered from a home center gain new purpose in this multifunctional bonus room. OPPOSITE: A canvas garden satchel transports supplies for work projects.

- **Ample desk drawers and a smartly configured wall cabinet,** *opposite,* make efficient use of a tight space and transform a small niche into a storage-savvy corner office for adults. ● **Wide pocket doors,** *left,* open to the adjoining family room, enabling the homeowners to meld the two living spaces or separate them and create a noise barrier when needed. ● **A pantry cabinet,** *above left,* is repurposed as media storage. Pullout trays make movie selection and viewing a snap. ● **Open cubbies and spice drawers,** *above right,* corral office supplies. Labeled pulls make identifying drawer contents easy. ● **A pint-size desk,** *below,* gives little ones their own space to create art, crafts, and inevitable messes. The quartz countertop is durable, stain-resistant, and easy to clean. As kids grow, the desk can be raised to standard height by installing cabinet feet under the vertical spice drawers and removing the lowest row of upper drawers.

Two are better than one: With a desk for grown-ups and one for kids, little ones can spill at will and not worry about making a mess of Mom and Dad's work space.

● **Magnetic paint and magnets** on the side of the cabinet, *opposite,* display kids' art, while quiet-close drawers under the upholstered window seat keep little fingers safe. ● **Wall-mount clipboards,** *left,* enable easy rotation of a kid's latest masterpieces or more traditional prints. ● **The sofa** converts to a queen-size bed, *above left,* when the room hosts overnight guests. The circular play table gets a quick transformation as well. ● **Easy-to-add amenities,** such as a single-cup coffeemaker and local road map, *above right,* help guests feel instantly at home.

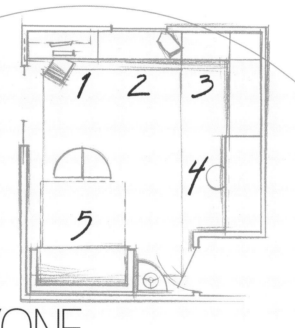

IN THE ZONE
Wrapping two walls of this den with cabinets yields lots of function.

1 work
Kitchen cabinets configured as a desk act as a hardworking center for family communications, bill paying, and homework projects.

2 relax
An upholstered window seat can store blankets or toys. The feature also gives the room extra seating without taking up floor space.

3 watch
TV, DVD player, and loads of movies fill the upper portion of this corner cabinet for easy viewing anywhere in the room.

4 create
This kid-friendly area is outfitted with a roll of art paper and scrubbable surfaces. The desk height can be adjusted as kids grow.

5 play/sleep
Flexible furnishings— notably a sleeper sofa and a four-piece repositionable table— make this area fun for kids and comfy for guests.

blending utility
with beauty

Short on space but long on organization, a tiny workroom serves many functions.

Small but mighty, this 6×9-foot workroom is proof that efficient storage and organization are more important than size. The diminutive space handily serves as laundry room, home office, family command center, and gift-wrapping station with carefully thought-out and clearly defined storage solutions. Wraparound countertops unite the U-shape configuration that has cabinets and open shelving below and more cabinets and shelves, a magnet board, and a pegboard above.

A washer, dryer, and sink are grouped along one wall to keep all laundry functions together. Cabinets hold detergent and fabric softener. Counter space is clean and uncluttered for folding clothes that can then be deposited in clearly labeled baskets on nearby shelves. Above the laundry area, open shelves display books and magazines, while a pegboard with hooks and baskets corrals everything needed to wrap gifts.

A shelf installed above the window on the far wall uses every inch of space, holding decorative accessories and additional baskets for hide-away storage. A slim countertop in the office area—just big enough for a laptop computer and a few desktop accessories—is flanked by floor-to-ceiling cabinets that hold a printer, files, and precisely labeled cubbies for coupons, keys, and other easily misplaced items. Above the desk, a magnet board displays shopping lists, notes, appointments, and schedules, with room for family photos. And, last but not least, there is even space in the workroom to stash the family pet's dog food.

THIS PHOTO: The laundry area—with a washer, a dryer, and a sink for hand-washing delicates—is supplemented by cabinet storage and countertop space for sorting and folding clothes. OPPOSITE: Small drawers, file holders, and lots of labels turn an ordinary cabinet into an efficient bill-paying station.

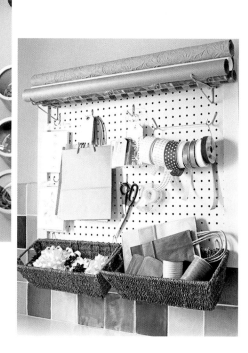

- **A combination of open shelves** and closed cupboards, *opposite,* keeps everything in its place in this multifunctional workroom.
- **A handy clipboard** with stain-removal tips, *left,* hangs inside a cabinet door, an often-overlooked storage spot. • **A magnet board,** *above left,* brings together schedules, appointments, and shopping lists to keep the whole family running smoothly. Small metal containers keep paper clips and rubber bands at hand. • **A wall-hung rectangle of pegboard,** *above right,* becomes an efficient gift-wrapping station, with all supplies neatly organized and within reach. Cards, ribbon, scissors, and tape hang from hooks, while brackets keep rolls of wrapping paper accessible and baskets contain bows and bags.

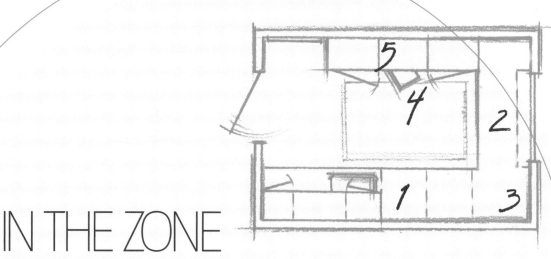

IN THE ZONE
Specially outfitted areas let a small space do many things efficiently.

1 wash
A washer, dryer, and deep sink packed into a tiny space ensure that wash day is a breeze. Laundry supplies and instructions tuck away in upper cabinets.

2 fold
A U-shape countertop extends over the washer and dryer, providing ample space for folding. Labeled baskets under the window make sorting clean garments easy.

3 wrap
A pegboard outfitted with hooks for paper, bags, cards, and ribbons organizes everything for great gift-wrapping. Baskets gather smaller tools and bows.

4 work
A small slice of open counter offers just enough space for a laptop and a few files. A tower-style built-in houses a printer, paper, and other office necessities.

5 organize
A wall-mount magnet board behind the desk extends to the ceiling, keeping clutter off counters and displaying lists, notes, and schedules for the entire family.

a superstar
storeroom

This efficient pantry organizes a household—and doubles as a crafter's dream.

This 7×5-foot workroom just steps away from the kitchen combines passions for organization and crafts. The room boasts banks of contrasting semicustom cabinets, each designed to house a vast array of supplies—from skeins of yarn and spools of colorful ribbon to silver serving trays and sacks of potatoes.

For an easy-to-clean craft-focused zone, scrubbable white cabinets were selected. Overhead cupboards hide less attractive crafting essentials, while flanking tower-style shelves rely on small drawers and fabric-lined baskets. The 2-foot-deep work surface straddles a small lap drawer with a trio of larger pantry drawers on either side. Chocolate-brown cabinets, including one outfitted with a bar for hanging table linens, border the central unit.

More chocolate cabinets on the room's opposite side serve as a handsome buffet. Frosted-glass upper doors not only keep serving pieces dust-free but also make them easy to identify. Nearby, tall vertical tray shelves store platters and baking pans. Just below are open shelves for beverages, and beneath those, a wire pullout bin for bulk foods and paper products. Additional wire pullouts corral wine bottles and bags of snacks, while drawers with vintage-style pulls keep linens tidy.

THIS PHOTO: A white-painted, Shaker-inspired workstation organizes an abundance of colorful wraps and ribbons. OPPOSITE: Acrylic bins make picking the perfect bow easy.

• **A hanging rod** designed to hold clothing, *opposite,* is repurposed to place multiple ribbon spools at a crafter's fingertips. • **Partial fronts on 24-inch-deep drawers,** *left,* hint at the contents and extend fully to reveal what's inside.
• **Cardboard take-out boxes,** *above left,* are a fresh alternative to gift bags; they store flat and also help organize small bows, enclosure cards, and trimmings.
• **Square drawers with vintage-style pulls,** *above right,* open to reveal cloth-lined baskets of cards and stationery. • **A T-slat wall behind the work surface,** *below,* makes adjusting the height of pegs and bins a cinch.

A mix of cabinet sizes, styles, shapes, and finishes helps this room avoid a boring, uniform look and offers targeted storage for specific items.

● **A massive walnut-stained unit,** *opposite,* fills the other half of the room, organizing items such as dishes, serving pieces, linens, and culinary staples. ● **Adjustable open shelves,** *left,* can quickly be repositioned to suit the size of items from cereal boxes and condiments to tea service and fine crystal.
● **Stainless-steel wire baskets,** *above left,* glide out for easy access to linens, snacks, or produce.
● **A heavy-duty extending wire-rack system,** *above right,* categorizes various vintages.

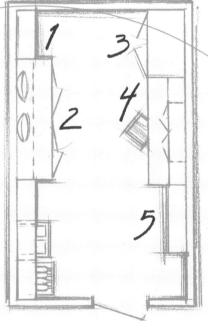

IN THE ZONE

This pantry makes the most of a narrow room's two long walls.

1 file
Five equally sized vertical slots sort platters, trays, and baking sheets. Positioning the slots at eye level makes selecting the right item easier.

2 protect
A pair of glass-front upper cabinets feature a subtle etched leaf pattern, ensuring large serving pieces are visible yet remain dust-free.

3 hang
This armoire-style corner cabinet houses two adjustable clothing rods that are outfitted with heavy-duty hangers for keeping table linens crisp.

4 create
The crafty contents of baskets, bins, drawers, and cabinets surround a central work surface. The T-slot wall can be reconfigured as needs change.

5 shelve
Just a few steps from the kitchen, this area functions as a cookbook library. The bottom shelf holds bolts of wrapping paper in a wicker wastebasket.

welcoming
workstation

Savvy storage solutions transform a quiet corner into a multitasking marvel.

Carving a niche in your home for all manner of business—from bookkeeping and bill paying to scrapbooking and archiving your budding Picasso's masterpieces—requires just a small amount of space. This hardworking home office occupies only a 6×8-foot corner but is packed with ideas for dynamic, good-looking function.

Before creating the work space, the homeowner considered activities she planned to do there, the size and scope of her office equipment, general lighting requirements, and whether she planned to hold meetings in the office. A key strategy for maximizing storage was putting the two available walls to work: Open shelving, a shallow cabinet with pegs, a magnetic board, and a wall-mounted clipboard significantly reduce desktop clutter. Less-used items are stashed on the highest shelves, while little necessities such as paper clips and thumbtacks are close at hand in magnetic containers..

A basic writing desk and two ready-to-assemble bookcases topped with medium-density fiberboard (MDF), all painted a creamy white, create an L-shape workstation. The printer/fax/copier and work folders fill the interior case, while books and magazines are easily available in the other.

● **A plank of medium-density fiberboard (MDF),** *opposite,* links a no-frills writing desk and two off-the-rack bookcases; creamy white paint unifies the pieces. ● **A small open bookcase,** *left,* boosts the storage capability under the desk and houses a printer/copier/fax and less-used files.

● **Inventive retasked containers,** *above left,* including flea-market kitchen accessories and a lunch box, hold gift-wrapping flourishes and stickers. ● **A wall-mount bathroom cabinet with pegs and cubbies,** *above right,* keeps small items such as notepads, stationery, and a container of pens within easy reach.

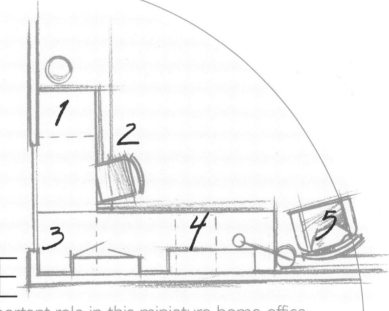

IN THE ZONE

Every surface plays an important role in this miniature home office.

1 connect
A magnetic memo board and wall-mount clipboard hung at one end of the workstation give family members two easy ways to leave each other messages.

2 work
Under a window, the main desk sits in the room's brightest spot. Holes drilled in the back of the desk drawers accommodate electronic devices.

3 stow
Undercounter bookcases with adjustable shelves enable hardworking office electronics and project files to be close at hand and out of sight.

4 access
A mix of open shelves, glass-door cabinets, hooks, and cubbies lining the largest wall keeps tools and supplies for a range of tasks quickly accessible.

5 host
A cozy wicker chair creates a secondary work spot—or an inviting place to kick back with a book at day's end— at this edge of the workstation.

1

smart solutions
front entries

Create the ideal landing spot for all those books, bags, coats, and more.

1 LOOK UP, THINK DIFFERENT
A mix of open and door-front modular cubes stacks vertically on one side of the front door. On the other side, a repurposed shadow box houses keys, and a ladle gathers loose change.

2 HOOKED ON HOOKS Line an entry wall with wainscoting that has a scrubbable paint or stain finish. Install a series of hooks at alternating heights to accommodate different bits of gear—and differently sized family members.

3 GO DOOR FREE Make a coat closet easy to access by removing doors. Paint the closet interior a contrasting color, then outfit the space with collapsible bins for balls and shoes, low-mounted wire racks for bags, and higher pegs for jackets and scarves.

smart solutions
garages

Exceptional durability and function give this hardworking space a special beauty.

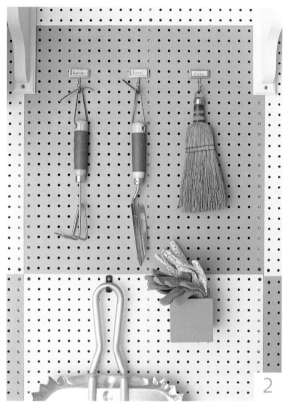

1 HEAVY DUTY When outfitting a garage for storage, don't skimp. Invest in durable metal cabinets with industrial locking casters, at least one surface with a hardwood countertop, and a heavy-duty wall-slat system with hangers specially designed to hold garden tools, ladders, shelving, and more.

2 SQUARED PEGS Use tape and two shades of contrasting paint to transform a basic pegboard wall into a colorful grid. Rather than measuring, just use the evenly spaced holes to guide your design.

3 REPURPOSED GEAR Put storage accessories from other rooms to work in the garage: Rout holes in wooden display shelves to hold hand tools, fill magnetic spice containers with nuts and bolts, and thread rolls of tape and wire onto a wooden suit hanger.

smart solutions
mudrooms
Leave your cares—and clutter—at the door with these efficient spaces.

1 SLIM SUBSTITUTIONS To equip an entry area with limited floor space to function as a hardworking mudroom, start by lining the walls with scrubbable beaded board. (As a bonus, cover a section of wall with chalkboard paint for a message zone.) Then hang a series of hooks, rather than cabinets, to hold gear.

2 SIT ON IT Incorporate adequate wall space, and a run of low storage compartments for boots and shoes can double as a dressing bench or landing spot for shopping bags.

3 CREATIVE CUBBIES Make the most of the often unused cubic feet under a staircase by carving out open shelves or bins.

4 GROW WITH IT Install adjustable shelves and repositionable hooks in storage lockers so you can reconfigure them as needed.

drippy details Wetness is unavoidable in a mudroom. Choose a gloss or semigloss finish for painted surfaces and stone, tile, or vinyl flooring. Include plastic or stainless-steel drainage racks and trays to catch messy boots and shoes.

smart solutions
hideaway desks

With creativity, the tiniest of spaces can accommodate a well-equipped home office.

2

3

1 DYNAMO DINING A shallow wall cabinet of supplies transforms a breakfast nook into an ideal spot for homework projects or telecommuting. Wall-mount vases corral office supplies or display bunches of flowers.

2 CLOSED-DOOR POLICY Paint, a pendant light, bulletin boards, and various ready-to-assemble storage units transform a bedroom closet into a complete office. Use table legs and wall brackets to convert a prefinished wall shelf into a slim desk.

3 DIVIDING DUTY A wheeled partition with cubbies and a flip-down writing surface can swing into this living room for big projects or hug the wall when groups gather in the space.

if you only have one hour...
Create a mobile mini office by filling a box, basket, or accordion file with essential office and paper supplies. Place the mini office near the sofa, the dining table, your bed—or any place you like to jot down notes.

smart solutions
memo stations

For on-the-go households, a communication center keeps everyone connected.

1 MIX IT UP Combine semicustom kitchen cabinets (available at home centers) into a wall of family-friendly storage. Choose a cabinet line with various drawer inserts and special features that can be repurpsed to hold office supplies.

2 WIRE WONDER Mount desktop file bins to a wall to function as easy drop boxes for papers or project supplies.

3 DOUBLE DUTY Make colorful clipboards work extra hard by hanging them on a wall and attaching hooks for bags and coats.

4 CLOSET CASE Introduce a hardworking message station into a room by removing a section of closet doors and installing a counter-height ledge. Wrap a piece of cork in fabric and frame it with decorative trim for a memo board that resembles wall art.

delightful delegation Whatever form command central takes in your home, assign a specific drawer, box, bin, filing slot, or clip to each family member. Label each spot clearly with a sticker or tag so everyone knows who's responsible for the contents.

1

smart solutions
by the desk

Getting more done in your home office begins with an organized desktop.

2

3

4

1 WRAP AROUND Top a U-shape desk with a bank of shallow cabinets to double its function. Install a kitchen backsplash rail system to hold bins, memo boards, and bulletin boards.

2 STORAGE SHOE-IN Fill the cubbies of a ready-to-assemble closet shoe organizer with jars and canisters of office supplies.

3 SERVING PIECES Organize art or office supplies in multipiece serving sets, such as this vintage aluminum tumbler set.

4 RETRO REUSE Use flea market tins and lunch boxes to organize media and supplies. Rely on cardboard document boxes to protect papers; label boxes to highlight specific projects or owners.

basket case Substitute flat baskets for plastic "in" and "out" boxes. Use deeper baskets for mail, magazines, and projects. Consider divided baskets designed for flatware to organize office supplies. Unify mismatched baskets with a coat of spray paint.

smart solutions on the wall

With a little planning a wall can organize more than framed pictures.

1 LAYER ON OPTIONS A fabric-wrapped corkboard and a spray-painted metal tray casually rest on top of a bookcase to function as versatile memo boards.

2 ON THE SKINNY Make the most of a sliver of wall—in an entryway or on the side of a built-in—by hanging letter holders and hooks.

3 CRISSCROSS Create a floor-to-ceiling French memo board by attaching grosgrain ribbon with upholstery tacks. Use the wall to hold reminders and bits of inspiration.

4 BRACKETS AND BINS Outfit a 4x8-foot panel of slatwall (a staple of retail displays, now available at home centers) with adjustable shelves and wire racks to organize books, files, and office supplies.

run a rotating gallery Resist the urge to display every photo, cartoon, and clever clipping you have on a bulletin board. Instead, select a few items at a time to tack up. Change the items every other week or once a month.

14 fast fixes: laundry room

Wash away clutter by assembling the elements of a multipurpose laundry center.

solutions:

1. Choose a versatile supply cabinet with doors and movable shelves.

2. Replace solid doors with pegboard, which boosts ventilation and storage options.

3. Gather tips and special care instructions with a clamp affixed to the cabinet door.

4. Safely store a hot iron in a wall-mount cooling rack.

5. Use wire hooks to create dedicated hanging spots for lint rollers and other tools.

6. Organize an array of linen waters on a lazy Susan.

7. Attach a collapsible clothes rod to the cabinet's underused side.

8. Get more from the hamper by topping it with a folding board or padded ironing board.

9. Sort laundry in a multibag rolling hamper and speed up wash day.

10. Opt for smaller bottles of concentrated detergent and softener to save space.

11. Catch messy spills and drips from detergents with a plastic tray.

12. Squeeze in more storage for dryer sheets by attaching an undershelf wire bin.

13. Repurpose pencil canisters as door-mount holders for brushes and spot cleaners.

14. Use labeled flip-top jars to collect pocket finds, clothespins, and sewing accessories.

resources

Following are some manufacturers and retailers that offer storage products to help you begin organizing your home.

Bed Bath and Beyond
800/462-3966
bedbathandbeyond.com
Storage and home organization products

Better Homes and Gardens Furniture Collection by Universal Furniture
877/804-5535
bhgfurniture.com
Home storage furniture

Bungalow
866/740-5886
bungalowco.com
Storage and home organization products

Buttoned Up
734/477-5020
getbuttonedup.com
Home office and organization products

California Closets
888/336-9709
californiaclosets.com
Custom home storage systems

Case Logic
888/666-5780
caselogic.com
Media storage systems

CB2
888/606-6252
cb2.com
Storage and home organization products

Chiasso
877/244-2776
chiasso.com
Storage and home organization products

ClosetMaid
800/874-0008
closetmaid.com
Modular home storage systems you can install yourself

The Container Store
888/266-8246
containerstore.com
Storage and home organization products

Cost Plus World Market
877/967-5362
worldmarket.com
Storage and home organization products

Crate & Barrel
800/967-6696
crateandbarrel.com
Storage and home organization products

Easy Track/ORG
800/562-4257
easytrack.com
homeorg.com
Modular home storage systems

Easyclosets.com
800/910-0129
easyclosets.com
Custom home storage systems you can install yourself

Ecotots
866/490-9800
ecotots.com
Storage furniture for children

Enclume
877/362-5863
enclume.com
Kitchen storage furniture

Eurway
877/938-7929
eurway.com
Ready-to-assemble storage furniture

Exposures
800/222-4947
exposuresonline.com
Photo display and storage products

Garnet Hill
800/870-3513
garnethill.com
Home storage products

Gladiator Garage Works
866/342-4089
gladiatorgw.com
Garage organization products

The Great American Hanger Co.
800/573-1445
hangers.com
Clothing storage and organization products

Home Decorators Collection
877/537-8539
homedecorators.com
Storage and home organization products

Home Depot USA, Inc.
800/553-3199
homedepot.com
Home organization and home improvement products; design consultation services

Howard Miller
616/772-7277
howardmiller.com
Home storage furniture

IKEA
800/434-4532
ikea.com
Ready-to-assemble storage solutions
and furniture

Improvements
800/634-9484
improvementscatalog.com
Storage and home organization products

JCPenney
800/322-1189
jcpenney.com
Home storage furniture

J.K. Adams
800/451-6118
jkadams.com
Kitchen storage products and systems

Kangaroom Storage
800/341-9159
kangaroomstorage.com
Storage and home organization products

KraftMaid Cabinetry
800/571-1990
kraftmaid.com
Semi-custom kitchen cabinets and
storage systems

Land of Nod
800/933-9904
landofnod.com
Storage products for kids

Lillian Vernon
800/901-9291
lillianvernon.com
Home storage products

OfficeMax
800/283-7674
officemax.com
Home office organization and home
storage products

Organize.com
800/600-9817
organize.com
Storage and home organization products

Organized A to Z.com
888/989-2869
organizedatoz.com
Storage and home organization products

OXO
800/545-4411
oxo.com
Kitchen storage products

PBteen
866/472-4001
pbteen.com
Storage and home organization products

Pottery Barn
888/779-5176
potterybarn.com
Storage and home organization products

Racor
800/783-7725
racorinc.com
Garage storage solutions

Restaurant Source
800/460-8402
restaurantsource.com
Food storage products

Restoration Hardware
800/910-9836
restorationhardware.com
Home organization products

Rev-a-Shelf
800/626-1126
rev-a-shelf.com
Storage inserts for cabinets

Rubbermaid
866/271-9249
rubbermaid.com
Storage and home organization products

Sauder
800/523-3987
sauder.com
Ready-to-assemble storage furniture

See Jane Work
877/400-5263
seejanework.com
Home office and organization products

Simple Human
877/988-7770
simplehuman.com
Storage and home organization products

Space Savers
800/849-7210
spacesavers.com
Storage and home organization products

Stacks & Stacks
800/761-5222
stacksandstacks.com
Home, office, and garden organization products

Staples
800/782-7537
staples.com
Home office organization products

Storables
866/227-0092
storables.com
Storage and home organization products

Target
800/800-8800
target.com
Storage and home organization products

Thomasville Cabinetry
thomasvillecabinetry.com
Semi-custom kitchen cabinets

Tupperware
800/366-3800
order.tupperware.com
Food storage products

Umbra
800/387-5122
umbra.com
Storage and home organization products

West Elm
888/922-4119
westelm.com
Storage and home organization products

index

A

appliances, kitchen, 51, 59–60
armoires
    bathrooms, 131, 143
    kitchen, 39

B

backsplashes, 54–55
baking center, 39, 60
bar area
    beverage center, 32
    entertainment stations, 86–87
    stemware, 57
barware containers, for bathroom
    storage, 131
bathrooms, 125–149
    clean and clutter-free, 126–131
    freestanding storage, 142–143
    linen closets, 144–145
    master suites, 100–101
    shower storage, 135, 136, 146–147
    streamlined organization for, 132–135
    toiletries, 138–139
    towel bars, 140–141
    vanities, 129, 131, 136–137, 143, 148
bedrooms, 92–123
    bedside storage, 110–113
    built-ins for, 96, 97, 99, 101, 114–115
    children's rooms, 102–104
    closets, 103, 106–109, 116–122
    efficient storage for, 98–101
    floor plans, 97, 101, 104
    master suites, 94–97, 98–99
    planning for, 15
bedside storage, 110–113
bench seating
    bedrooms, 97
    living spaces, 65, 82–83
    showers, 147
bins
    cooking storage, 29
    gift-wrapping stations, 163
    silverware, 57
    wall storage, 185

bookcases
    bedrooms, 111, 114
    living spaces, 73, 80–81, 82
    work spaces, 171
boxes
    color-coded fabric boxes, 104
    gift-wrapping, 165
    hinge-top, 83
    lidded, 121
    translucent, 71
breakfast nooks
    function of, 19–20
    planning for, 12–13
    as work spaces, 179
built-in storage
    bathrooms, 130, 134
    bedrooms, 96, 97, 99, 101, 114–115
    kitchens, 47
    shelving, 71, 77, 114–115
    wall storage in bathrooms, 137
bump-out media, 115

C

cabinets
    bathrooms, 128, 131, 135, 136, 138, 139,
        143, 145
    bedrooms, 111, 114–115
    as bench seating, 83
    children's bedrooms, 104
    comfort/convenience of, 31
    inside cabinets, 52–53
    kitchen, 38, 41
    laundry rooms, 159
    living spaces, 73
    media storage, 79
    memo stations, 181
    narrow, 49
    open, 81
    pantries, 45
    work spaces, 153, 155
carts, 77, 143
chests of drawers, 75, 85
children's bedrooms, 102–104
china hutches
    kitchens, 29, 50
    living spaces, 84–85

clipboards, 157, 161, 181
closets
    bathrooms, 145
    children's, 119
    for creative activities, 122
    dressing islands, 116
    floor plans, 109
    front entries, 173
    as home offices, 179
    linen, 144–145
    living spaces, 81
    organizers for, 117–121
    seating in, 103
    shared, 106–109
coat racks, 103
coffee center, 59
communication center, 11. *See also*
    memo stations
cooking, 24–29
    bins, 29
    cook stations, 46–47
    floor plans, 29
    islands, 27
    shelving, 25, 26, 28
cords, 79
corner bookcases, 81
corner storage, in showers, 147
crafting storage, 122, 161, 162–167
cubbies, 49
    bathrooms, 137
    bedrooms, 97, 101
    as hideaway desks, 179
    kitchen, 35, 49
    mudrooms, 177
    work spaces, 155, 171

D

dens, 157
desks, 155, 171
    desktop organization, 183
    drawers, 154
    hideaway desks, 179–180
    memo stations, 181–182
    See also work spaces